Hab—His Life and Times

Hab—His Life and Times

Harry Owen Jackson

VANTAGE PRESS
New York

Cover design by Sue Thomas

FIRST EDITION

All rights reserved, including the right of
reproduction in whole or in part in any form.

Copyright © 2003 by Harry Owen Jackson

Published by Vantage Press, Inc.
516 West 34th Street, New York, New York 10001

Manufactured in the United States of America
ISBN: 0-533-14374-8

Library of Congress Catalog Card No: 2002092966

0 9 8 7 6 5 4 3 2 1

To my brother, Lee M. Jackson, my guide and counselor always

Contents

Introduction ix

My Childhood	1
My First Job	20
Country School	27
Harry and Mildred	30
High School	39
The Junior-Senior Banquet	46
Senior Year	49
Model T	52
Home Life	58
Time for College	64
Sophomore Year	74
Summer in Michigan	93
Senior Year, Continued	99
Post-College	101
Finding a Home	106
Work Woes	109
A New Job	118
Preparing for the Service	125
Life after the Navy	144
Summer of 1949	150
A New Job	154
Family Travels	169
Back Home Again	182
Ken Grows Up	189
Time for a Move	200

Introduction

My story begins with a young woman, a passenger on a ship inching into its berth in the harbor at Baltimore. The woman had given her name as Jackson, and was to be indentured for seven years, presumably to pay for her passage. The name . . . Jackson . . . was an assumed name. Her true family-name was known only to her son, William Henry Jackson, but he never divulged it to anyone.

The woman served her indenture in Maryland in or near Fredericks City, where William Henry was born. He was also "bound out" to a farmer near Fredericks City. The farmer was to feed, clothe, and educate him, but was lax on all counts. After a few years, he ran away and finally found employment with another farmer for eight dollars a month. Later, he worked for another farmer for twelve dollars a month, enough that he saved enough money to buy a team and wagon so that he could go into the freight-hauling business somewhere in Pennsylvania.

William Henry Jackson was my great-grandfather. He and a brother came to Logan County in Illinois in 1856 by way of the Chicago and Alton Railway, and for ten dollars an acre, purchased a hundred and sixty acres in West Lincoln Township, about six miles northwest of Lincoln—which eventually became the county seat.

I have no information about their reason for selecting this location, but it is possible that news of the rich black soil and the rapid settlement reached them and sounded good to them.

Eventually, William married and had a son, Levi, one of ten children. Levi lived on the farm until 1921. In his later years, William lived with Levi and his wife, Lucinda Jane Musick, until his death.

My father was the eldest son of Levi and Lucinda Jane. His name was Harry Owen Jackson, and I was given the same name.

My mother's family were of the Mennonite faith and probably had their roots with members who were part of the migration from Switzerland. Some of them, after a sojourn in Holland, emigrated to the new world, most settling in Ohio and Pennsylvania.

My mother always claimed to be Pennsylvania Dutch and a note of pride seemed to be noticeable when she mentioned it. My maternal great-grandmother was of the sect known as the Dunkards (or Donkards), also known as the River Brothers.

My maternal grandfather, Valentine Nicodemus, married Fannie Wriggle and blessed the world with two sons and four daughters.

My mother's name was Dora Viola. I always thought that it was a beautiful name, probably, in part, because I loved her so much, as did everyone that knew her. In later years, she was known as "Aunt Dode" to the dozens of relatives and friends who loved to eat at her table.

She was born in a little village named Burtonview, just a hop and a jump west of Lincoln.

When my father and mother were married, they were part of that section of the population that were needed on the farms, especially if the owner didn't have children old enough to do the manual labor. Dad worked for several years, and did well. Dad and Mother's first child was a daughter, Clarice Naomi, who was born in 1898. A son, Lee Martin, was born in 1900, and another daughter, Frances Musick (I think she later changed the spelling to Musich) was born in 1905.

In 1907, Dad worked for a farmer named Klatt. This was during the time that the great cattle ranches in the southwest were breaking up into smaller units and "land agents" (Mom hated them) were advertising for farmers to come west. There was considerable talk about the rich land (true) and the good climate (also true), but with reservations such as dust storms, blue northers and no rain when you needed it. Middle-western corn belt farmers were not the best candidates for dry-land farming. Hundreds tried it and failed. A minority lived through it, and some stuck it out and got rich.

Mr. Klatt bought 1,280 acres in Moore County near Middle Well, a little community tucked into what had been a part of the LS Ranch and near the border of the famous XIT Ranch, which had its headquarters in Channing, fifteen miles south. The XIT headquarters building is still standing and can be seen in Channing.

This part of the Texas panhandle is also in that part of Texas referred to as the "High Plains" and the "Staked Plains." Let me say right here that, bad or good, love it or hate it, I, for one, love it and I am proud to have been Texas born.

Mr. Klatt went to Texas to see what he was getting for his money. I don't know what his reaction was, but he offered Dad a partnership, asking him to come down and operate the ranch/farm. Dad accepted the offer. What a difference a stroke of the pen can make in the lives of generations to come!

Clarice was nine years old and Lee was seven. Frances was going on two, and judging by what I have been told, none of them were enthused about the prospects.

Dad had gone before to meet Mr. Klatt at the ranch and to take care of the items that had come by freight train. When the family arrived, Dad met them at the station in Channing. He had a wagon to haul the family and the household goods out to the ranch. The team and wagon was the only means of transportation; there were no roads in Moore County at that time. There were only trails made by buggy or farm wagon; some of the plainer ones were cattle trails made by the ranches driving their herd to the railroad corral and terminating at the Channing Pens.

The wind was blowing, Texas-style, and carrying its share of the high plains' dust with it, making the trail invisible part of the time. When it wasn't, you just headed across the Plains in what you hoped was the right direction.

Clarice had a little rocking chair, which was one of her prized possessions. Apparently, it was not tied securely, and the wind blew it out of the wagon and across the plains. They hunted for it, but it was never found.

It was not a pleasant drive. Fifteen miles under those conditions was pure torture, but like most trails, it had an end, right at the gate of the picket fence that surrounded the yard.

It was not a lawn. There was not a blade of grass in the entire enclosure. Clarice remembers Dad saying, "What a hell of a place to bring a family to."

The trip between the ranch and Channing was made many times in the fourteen years that my family lived there. There were times of pleasure and pride; times of storm and strife . . . life at its fullest, and death at its most tragic.

My sister, Clarice, tells about the deaths of little Edith Ellen and Cecil.

On the Sunday preceding little Edith Ellen's illness, Mother held her on her lap during the church service. She reached up and played with a curl that was available under Mother's hat, gently pulling it, then pretending to say, "Ouch!" though it was only a playtime squeal. It was a game that they had played before. Mom furnished the sound effects and the baby laughed.

Before the next Sunday, she had died of pneumonia.

There was no mortician in that part of the country, and no one was sure where they could get a coffin for a child.

One of the neighbors said he thought he knew where there was one. He took the team and wagon and drove twenty-two miles to Dumas, found a coffin suitable for a child, and brought it home.

Another neighbor, Mr. Fred Smith, and his wife, Nellie, laid her out, dressing her and folding her little hands. It was 1910.

She was buried in the cemetery at Dumas.

In 1913, a baby boy, Cecil Clyde, was stillborn and buried alongside Edith Ellen.

My mother tried a few times to tell me about these children, but could never say more than just a few words.

I have visited the graves twice since I have been old enough to appreciate the trials of those terrible ordeals on the High Plains.

My Childhood

The Moore County Pioneer

Vol. I; Dumas, Moore County, Texas; Friday, February 11, 1910

Edith Ellen Jackson was born July 1, 1909, and Jesus called her home February 2, 1910. She was seven months and three days of age.

Our darling babe has passed away, her sufferings are over. No more will her baby fingers clasp ours, no more will we be greeted by her welcoming smile.

It is oh, so hard to part, still, we do not question the will of the all-wise Father, for we know our loss is Edith's gain. She was baptized in the faith of the M. E. Church, September 12, 1909 by Brother John Creed.

Our Baby

> A precious one from us is gone,
> A voice we loved is stilled,
> A place is vacant in our home,
> Which never can be filled,
> God, in his wisdom, has recalled,
> The boon his love had given,
> And tho' the body slumbers here,
> The soul is safe in heaven.

To the neighbors and friends who so nobly assisted us in our hour of need, and for the sympathy extended to us in our sorrow, we extend our loving gratitude.

Though far from kith or kin, we have not wanted for anything that loving hearts and willing hands could give us.

—The Parents

As Lee tells of my arrival, he gives the impression that he was enthusiastic about it, even though I am sure that there were times when he wished that I was someplace else.

Sister Frances was ten years older than me, making me "the baby" of the family, as little sister Edith Ellen had died as a baby in 1910, and a boy, Cecil Clyde, was stillborn in 1913. Both of these children are buried in the city cemetery at Dumas, the graves cared for all these years and decorated for many years by dear friends, George and Gypsie Schlinkman, of Dumas.

After all of these tragic losses, one would expect a new baby to be spoiled rotten. No further comment except to say, "Lucky me!"

I was healthy enough, but Mother did not have enough milk. Fortunately, a neighbor lady, Annie MacFarland, had little Claude. He was my age and Annie had milk to spare. Clarice would take me down to her house every day for a square meal. Poor little Claudy didn't seem to suffer much. I did real well, although there was a time when I had to have bread soaked with coffee and a few drops of whiskey added for an upset stomach. I still have an occasional upset stomach . . . but I'm sure to have it only when there is an adequate supply of whiskey in the house.

Clarice says that she took me to Annie in our car, an EMF. I can't find anyone who remembers what an EMF was like. Lee always said the letters stood for "Every Morning Fix It." It was the first car in Moore County, and there were still no roads, only the usual trails, in 1916.

I think that most parents are conscious of the first word that an offspring says, but after a while, dismiss it as being of little importance, as more important events take their attention. In my family, you were reminded of your first word for the rest of your life . . . probably because it was connected to some event or behavior that led to the vocal manifestation.

When my folks came to the High Plains, they found some things to be quite different from those of the Illinois Prairie. One very noticeable feature was the wind. Not only did it blow more frequently, but it carried a good load of Texas soil with it. Another difference was the "quiet." Once in a while, a dog barked, a cow bawled, or a coyote yipped. Mostly, the only noise was the wind causing something to bang, clatter, thump or rattle. That was it . . . quiet.

My mother soon had enough of that, so she gently suggested to Dad that she wanted a clock that "struck." Mom's suggestions had a certain unspoken quality that gave certain, even if unconscious, results.

The next time Dad was in Channing, he went to Horn and Allen General Mercantile and purchased a Seth Thomas shelf clock that struck every hour and half hour.

My family has been listening to that clock strike for eighty-five years. The clock is now standing on a buffet on my son's living-dining room in Derby, Kansas. It is still keeping time and striking every hour.

As far as I know, I am the only member of my family whose first word was *clock*.

I must have had several toys, but there is only one that I remember playing with. It was a little red train engine, about twelve or fourteen inches long, made of wood, with wheels strong enough that I could straddle it and go scooting across the floor.

Lee worked really hard to get me to say "Fort Worth and Denver" but he finally gave up. I knew what a train was, having seen one coming through Channing, and we could see the smoking engines from our house if the wind wasn't blowing too hard and if the engine had enough of the right kind of coal.

We had a hired man one time who made a little windmill for me. It was great. He whittled the blades so that the wind would turn the wheel, just like the real one west of our house that pumped water into our overhead tank. Add a few stick horses, and I had it made. When they were younger, Lee and Clarice caught the little horned lizards that were common, put string on them for harnesses, and played like they were horses. I never got that far, and don't remember seeing any lizards, although I am sure there were some around.

I had another horse, too. About three feet from the kitchen wall, a pipe came up out of the ground, made a ninety degree turn, and through the wall into the kitchen. It was the underground pipe that ran to the overhead tank at the windmill and supplied water to the house.

The horizontal part made one of the finest cow ponies in the west, and I rode at least a million miles on the hurricane deck of that pipe: bareback, too.

We had several relatively close neighbors. Some were new, like us, but most of them had lived there for some time. Some of them were still Confederates at heart, and one family had lost a member in the war between the states. There was some cool resentment at first, but after we became acquainted, they accepted us.

Our local community center was the school and church. It was a school Monday to Friday; a Church on Sunday. It was called Middle Well, and was a positive factor in community relations.

Many of the families had to drive far enough that their noon meal was delayed, so there were frequent "Dinner on the Ground" affairs. It was "pot luck," each family brought something, table cloths were spread someplace out of the wind, and the food was placed where everyone could reach it.

Of course, every wife had her own dish that she considered especially good, so you had a pretty good idea of what would be available. Whether they were called Dinner on the Ground, Pot Luck, or Fetch In, the results were always the same; good food, fellowship, and friendship. Usually, you went home feeling better for having been there.

I cannot remember all of the families that we knew, but there were some that were important to us for one reason or another.

Clint and Corda Frye and daughter, Verna Mae, were frequent visitors at our house. Corda was from West-Central Illinois, the daughter of a prominent farmer near Ipava. Her maiden name was Lalicker (the *a* is long and the accent on the first syllable). I don't know any of Clint's family history before we knew him.

One of my fondest memories is of seeing Clint coming down the road ahead of a cloud of dust, turn into our lot, and circle around, heading out before he stopped. He drove what at that time was called a "jitney"; a single seat Model T Ford, probably a 1917 or 1918 model.

The cloth top was usually down and Clint's saddle was laid over the hood, as if it were a horse's back. In back of the seat there was a little box that Clint had made, about twenty-four or thirty inches wide and three feet long. It was Clint's version of a pick-up.

Verna Mae and I were playmates. I have been told (probably by Clarice, who was usually riding herd on me) that one day when I was about two, I started down the trail toward their house. I guess my family nearly had a fit because of the rattlesnakes, of which we had a good number. They certainly were dangerous and I was normally not let to run free out of the yard. I don't know if I was really headed for the Fryes' or if I just wanted to go on a hike. I guess that I had been cautioned about the snakes, because one day while playing in the yard, I started down the steps that led to our cave, or storm cellar. Stretched out on one of the steps was a healthy looking bullsnake. I hurried into the house and told Mom that there was a "Boo" out there. Mom grabbed her garden hoe and headed for the snake. I don't know the result other than I must have felt like a big game hunter. For killing snakes, you just can't beat a good garden hoe.

Corda had a brother, Chaunce (we called him Chant) Lalicker, who had recently lost his wife, leaving him with four children to look after. There were two boys, Maurice, who became my brother-in-law, and John, who certainly became a best friend, and two girls, Mary and Carolyn, who we always called Carrie. I always thought Carrie would make a wonderful girlfriend when I was about fourteen. The boys and Carrie were left with their grandparents and Chant brought Mary to Texas to live with Clint and Corda. About the same time, a niece of Clint's came to live with the Fryes for a while. Her name was Zella.

These young people visited with my brother and sisters, and that is where I came in. The soil in that area is very fine and easily blown about. It also gets in your eyes, in your nose, and in your ears. Since I was out in it most of the time, I had the dirtiest ears in the family. I also couldn't wash them, or at least, I didn't. Enter Frances. I loved her dearly, but I'll swear, she hated to wash my ears, and I hated to have her do it. She hurt! As far as I know, Mary didn't try it, probably because I raised such a storm.

Try Zella. You cannot believe the touch that girl had. Absolutely painless; even pleasant. I have never forgotten Zella Frye, and I won't. I saw her at a funeral a few years ago, but did not even mention ears. She probably would not remember.

One more story about Clint. He had to make the trip to town, probably Dumas, in his little jitney . . . or at least one like it. On the way home, about the middle of the afternoon, a rod bearing went out, leaving Clint afoot. He remembered that there was an oil-drilling crew working down the road a little way, so he started for it.

Surely enough, they had some babbit, a soft metal, which was easily worked. Clint rebuilt the bad bearing and drove on home.

That was not an easy job out in the middle of the plains, but is an example of the type of man who built our country; especially if he had a wife of like character to match.

The Fryes remained in Texas for several years after my folks moved to Illinois, and I remember my mother standing in the door, looking down the road, and saying, "Oh, I wish that I could see Clint and Cordy (she always called Clint's wife Cordy) come driving in!"

There came a time when she could.

I have mentioned the MacFarlands, but there is more! There were two families, Jim's and Claude's, but at the age of two or three, you don't pay much attention to the adults, except for Annie. I did see Annie in the summer of 1940, but did not see any of the children that I faintly remember. I remember Onamae, Fannie Ruth, Lawrence, and Ike . . . and of course, Claudy.

They were good neighbors, but the children were not old enough to spend a lot of time at our house, so I didn't get to know them well. I believe it was Claude that played a part in my family's life. What affected one of us, affected everyone. Mom saw to that.

A few years ago, Lee wrote the story of his life in longhand on a dimestore notebook. Not only did he write one for me, he made copies for his son, Davy, and possibly another for his daughter, Doris Della. In his account, he tells of one event that involved the Claude MacFarlands. Here is Lee's story of the horse, Quanah:

> A neighbor came to our house one afternoon, leading a little Indian pony named Quanah. His little daughter was ill with influenza, and he wanted me to ride Quanah for the doctor. He instructed me to hurry and not spare the horse.
>
> I rode that fifteen miles in an hour, contacted the doctor, and followed him to the sick child.
>
> It was nightfall when I got back home, so I kept the horse that night. I fed and watered him, all the time admiring him for his speed and stamina.
>
> The next day, I took Quanah back to the neighbor.
>
> First of all, I inquired about the sick girl and was told that she had responded nicely to the doctor's treatment, and that she had greatly improved.

I asked the man if he would sell the horse to me. He hesitated a moment, then said that he would sell him to me, but wouldn't sell him to anyone else. This made me very happy.

At the time, there was an established price for livestock. Calves were worth thirty dollars at weaning time, yearlings were sixty dollars and well-broken young horses were eighty dollars, so there was no quibbling about the price.

I bought him and never regretted it. I trained him to "run and walk," a gait that covered a lot of ground, but didn't tire the horse.

He became a good cutting horse. I did a lot of roping off him. He always seemed to know what to do.

I was offered a fabulous price for him, but I wouldn't sell him.

Quanah came to Illinois with us and was the first horse that I ever rode. There was not a dry eye in the family when we had to give him up.

Even though the country was sparsely settled and young folks were often several miles apart from their school, they did occasionally get together for parties and picnics. Sometimes, they went down to "the breaks," which was a kind of badlands area, with eroded gullies and other land forms. It was very pretty, but also very valuable to ranchers in the wintertime to protect stock from the blizzards and blue northers that swept the area. It was a good place to picnic and to take pictures with the new Kodak box cameras that were becoming so popular. A familiar expression was "to go Kodaking." Probably the most popular event was the picnic lunch. I don't really know for sure, as I was too young to go. One of my granddaughters, when she was a little tyke, was having a mild (?) debate with her mother, and I remember her saying, "It's not easy being a kid!" You surely were right, dear.

Dancing and card-playing were not allowed, but the young people got around that by having singing games such as Ju-tang and Skip-to-My-Lou. If there isn't a way, make it.

Clarice and Lee had one party, or at least one is all I remember. We had a piano in the parlor. I remember Julius Widling playing the music and the young folks singing while they played the game. They didn't dance, you know . . . just moved to the tune of the music.

Clarice and Lee attended the Middle Well school, which was about three miles from home. They rode horseback, tied the horse to a hitch rail, and let it stand there until it was time to go home. In later years, a shelter was built for the horses.

Occasionally, they got to use the buggy. Then, they had to unhitch the horse and tie it up as usual, but at recess time, they pushed the buggy out on the plains, put the top up, and using it as a sail, let the wind blow them back to the school yard. Of course, the school yard was not fenced in, but barbed wire was gradually enclosing the farms. The days of the open range were gone.

Clarice told me of her little White Rock chicken that was a favorite pet. It seems that the chicken would come to meet her when she came home from school, hop up onto the saddle, and ride back home. I forget what she said happened to Snow but you may be assured that she didn't end up in a pot or a skillet.

I have a few pages of this story devoted to the one-room school, but I want to quote some of Lee's experiences here. In Lee's *Life Story*, at age seventy-three, he wrote the following about his school days:

> Like for most small boys, school was a trying time for me. I went to a one-teacher school three miles from home. I was not the smartest kid nor was I the dumbest. I was always happy if my report card showed an eighty average. More often it didn't.
>
> The teacher, who was also janitor and coach, had ten grades so that didn't leave much time for class.
>
> High school was unheard of. We went to school until we were married or expelled, whichever came first. This means, of course, that there were always a few big boys in school, and they were known to cause trouble at times, although I never knew what I would call a really bad boy. This encouraged the directors to hire a male teacher. I liked that, and was more interested in my school work. The male teacher promoted sports and game activities.
>
> We purchased outdoor basketball equipment and a croquet set. We raised the money ourselves by sponsoring a basket festival and the young men of the community responded beautifully.

A note about another activity:

> Valentine's day was looked forward to from year to year.
> We always had a Valentine's party along with refreshments. We made our own valentines. I never saw a bought one until I was twenty

years old. They simply were not on the market in our locality and I would not have had the money to buy one if they had been.

Our valentines were made from sample wall paper books cut in the shape of a heart or some unique figure.

My sisters could paint well. They would sometimes paint a flower or a group of flowers on regular writing paper with a cute little verse inside.

I received a valentine from a little German girl one time. She had painted some violets on a heart-shaped piece of paper. Inside was this verse:

> I'm sending you this violet
> Because the two of us have met
> And hope that we, already yet
> Once more together, get.

I happen to know a thing or two about my brother that he was too modest to say in the above quote. He was very intelligent, a very deep thinker, and was very disappointed that he could not continue his education. Unlike me at that age, he wanted to be a teacher! Because he could not be, he made many sacrifices to make my teaching career possible. *Mil gracias, Hermano!* Believe me, the angels smiled at you!

There is much more that I could say about those childhood years. Although I did not experience these adventures, I grew up with them and they vicariously helped me to shape my character and my life.

Middle Well did not always have a male teacher. Clarice and Lee were fortunate to have one young lady. Her name was Chloe Danner and I barely remember her. Her sister, Helen, was a good friend of our family—married to Clyde Messenger, whom I was privileged to visit many years later. Chloe married Julius Widling, who came to our house and played the piano, including some of his own compositions.

In the summer of 1940, my parents and Joy and I drove to the old neighborhood and visited some of the former neighbors. Unfortunately, not many of them were left, but as a grown man, I listened to the conversations between those old friends. With them, I relived, in the very place where it happened, that part of their lives . . . and some of mine.

Nearly every farmer or rancher has to hire extra help to do seasonal work, such as harvesting the crops or, in our case, helping with the spring round-up, which involved the work of experienced cowboys.

One such boy was Norman Walke, a cowboy from Montana. He had been a guide in Glacier Park, and was experienced in all kinds of ranch work. He was with us for several months and left many impressions with me, as well as other members of the family. He seemed more like a member of the family than just a temporary worker, and I especially would have liked for him to stay with us; but "itchy feet" prevailed and he left. I never saw or heard from him again. One thing I learned was that no association is forever. It was a bitter lesson, and one I never forgot.

When he left us, he gave Lee a pair of silver-plated spurs, and left a pair of bearskin mittens with me to wear when I got big enough. I never grew into those mittens, but I did have them for years. I took them to school one time for "show and tell" time, but the other kids were not impressed. I put them in my dresser drawer when I got home, but they disappeared and were never found. Lee's spurs were gone, too.

Soon after he left us, Clarice married a young man named Herbert Cecil. When their first child was born, he was named Norman, after Norman Walke.

There has always been music in our home. My mother played an accordian, and Dad an alto horn. Clarice and Lee had taken piano lessons and would practice on the big, heavy upright piano in the living room. Dad, Mom, and Clarice sometimes sang hymns. I don't remember Lee and Frances singing them, although both had beautiful voices. I would sing, too, but not hymns. I still don't sing them, and won't listen to them unless I have to, like in church.

Lee never played the piano, but played the guitar well. He could play the violin well, too, but didn't like it.

Frances was too young to take piano lessons when Clarice and Lee did, but when they had finished their practice time, Frances would sit down and play their lesson "by ear." She never did learn to read music, but she had a beautiful touch and perfect timing. If I were blindfolded and listened to a group of pianists, I believe that I could tell which one was Frances.

Several years later, when we returned to Illinois, the old upright piano came with us, and as long as there were kids at home or near, the piano in the parlor could be heard.

I didn't know much about the war—World War I, that is. I learned a great deal about the second one. All I knew was that men were shooting each other, and that Mom was real mad at some old geezer named Kaiser Bill in Germany and France, wherever that was . . . or what it was. It must be bad if they had to shoot each other. In the years my folks lived in Texas, I don't think that any of us ever heard a gun shot! Where was the Wild and Wooley West?

Dad had done well on our little spread, and both he and Lee liked the life there. Not so with my mother and Clarice. Frances never committed herself, at least to me. It was like her to go along with the wishes of others. When she did make a choice, everyone would know it, and there was no turning back.

Grandpa (Levi) Jackson had begun to think seriously about retirement, and sometime in 1920 he wrote, wanting Dad to come back to Logan County. He had visited Texas, and was not favorably impressed with the chances of success with dry land farming.

More and more people were plowing up the sod that it had taken thousands of years to establish and were setting the stage for the Great Dust Bowl, nearly ten years in the future.

The decision was made. Dad sold our cattle to a Mr. Collins, who was very active in church work, and well thought of in the area around Dumas and Channing. He took the Collins note for ten thousand dollars. You guessed it, Collins went bankrupt. Dad was later paid a little over three hundred dollars in interest, and that was all he ever saw of his cattle money.

I never once heard a complaint, but we went into the depression years of the 1930s virtually broke.

I had a hard time figuring out what Illinois was. About the only thing that I remember was Mom trying to make me understand what a tree was. The only trees I had ever seen were some wild plum trees that grew along the Canadian River near Tascosa.

I remember being on the train, but only one isolated incident. It was something I didn't know existed, and was perfectly content to study from a distance . . . my first negro!

The only luggage that we had was what was on our backs, travel by train being the limiting factor. Travel by auto was even more difficult at that time. The plan was for Herbert to return to Texas later, and drive our Overland 90 to Illinois. That was a major accomplishment. Herbert made the trip without serious trouble.

I think the car may have been driven on local errands after that, but all I remember [about that] is that it was parked in a shed and left there until Dad finally traded it for a new 1921 Dodge touring car.

The Overland was usually driven with the top down, which I liked. One other incident stands out in my memory. One night, we were returning home after some neighborhood affair. It was winter and there was snow on the ground. Mom called my attention to the snow glistening in the headlights of the car. The headlights were very poor, and suddenly there was a bump. Dad had hit a cow. He got out of the car, looked, and said, "She wasn't hurt!"

One other incident occurred that summer. Clarice was driving across the plains, headed toward a gate which blocked the trail. Mom rode in the front seat with Clarice; Frances and I in the back. When we came to the gate, Frances got out and opened the gate, but failed to close the car door. After a time, that half-open door seemed to worry me, so I reached over and slammed it shut.

Clarice and Mom heard the door slam, thought Frances was in the car, and drove on. I let them drive on for some distance before they noticed that Frances was still back at the gate.

I was almost four years old at the time and should have responded more effectively. In fact, I don't know whether I ever did respond!

Brother Lee, in his life story, gives a somewhat different version of this event, but this is the way I remember it. The worst of it is, I didn't (and still don't) feel sorry! In fact, I think that I was glad that I was just a kid and too little to open and close wire gates.

The only livestock moved to Illinois was the horses and two collie ranch dogs, Ring and Buster. My brother-in-law, Herbert Cecil, rode with them. The household goods, clothing, and such were also shipped by train.

We made only one stop, Kansas City, where we spent one afternoon and night with friends, Ray and Corrine Nick, whom we had known in Texas. That was the night I saw my first show in a real theater. During the afternoon, Lee had an opportunity to see the sights. I don't know who was with him, but I remember how excited he was to have visited one of the Sears-Roebuck mail-order houses and watch the clerks hurrying around on roller skates, filling orders. That building is still standing and can be identified by the still-visible signs painted on the brick walls.

I only remember one other incident at the Nicks'. Dad went to the telephone to order a taxi to pick us up at four o'clock the next morning to take us to the train.

The journey to Illinois ended when the train stopped at the depot in Lincoln. We were met be a young man with a nice car, but it was dark. There was snow on the ground, and I was tired. For the first time, I got to see what grandparents were. I had never seen anything like that before, and I was looking for something different. I was a little bit disappointed to see that they were just like the rest of the grown-ups that I had known. I don't think that they were favorably impressed with me, either.

My life during the next few weeks is pretty much a blank. The old folks visited a lot, but in a few days, Grandpa Levi got in his old Buick with a horn that tooted when you squeezed a rubber bulb, and went to town.

When he came home that afternoon, he casually announced to Grandma that he had bought a house for them. The fact that Grandma had never seen it and knew nothing about it was immaterial.

It was many years before I was mature enough to understand how he felt about leaving the farm that his father and his uncle had broken out of the original prairie sod (the tall bluestem grass that made it, officially, a prairie), and the houses that they had built. Of course, he still owned the place, but he was facing a time when he was probably as insecure about the future as any time in his life.

Actually, Grandpa was only sixty-eight years old; not really old by today's standards, with modern machines to relieve him of the heavy work, but he was still in the "horse and buggy days," when even the heavy work was done by what Lee called the "armstrong method". That is, if something had to be moved, you picked it up and moved it. There was no machine to move it for you.

The sod of the Big Blue Stem was extremely difficult to break out, and since it had to be done initially with a walking plow, or, at best, with a sulky, it was a wonder that it could ever be plowed at all, but the Jackson boys did it. The result was a farm with some of the most fertile land in the world.

In spite of the hard work, there had been enjoyable times, too. Grandpa's hobby was going to "turkey shoots", where marksmen shot their rifles at targets, trying to win the first prize, which could be a turkey, a big cured ham, or some other reward of like value.

One time, Grandpa and Grandma went to a homecoming at Hartsburg, a nice little town about five miles north of the farm. One of the major attractions was a turkey shoot in which Grandpa participated. I didn't know whether he won the turkey or not, but he did draw some attention.

It seems that we had a president that was not real popular with the local residents, so they decided to hang him in effigy. Part of the program included a parade which included a fire engine from Lincoln, so they used the fire truck ladders to suspend a wire across the street between two high buildings and the effigy was hung on it.

After the celebration was over, they needed to take the poor president down, but the fire truck had gone back to Lincoln and they had no way to reach the wire. Grandpa studied the situation, and then said, "Boys, I believe I can get him down." He went to his buggy, got his rifle, and shot the wire in two.

The rifle was a Winchester '73, 32–20 calibur, which my grandmother gave to me when Grandpa died. It still shoots well, although the end of the barrel is slightly worn from the thousands of bullets that have been fired through it at turkeys.

It is one of my most valuable treasures and I will pass it on to my son, Kenneth Keith, who treasures it as I do. I hope that eventually some Jackson can stand to part with it and donate it to the Illinois State Museum at Springfield, Illinois.

After my grandparents and my great-grandfather moved to Lincoln, we were left to adjust to our new environment. Dad bought Grandpa's livestock and implements. Most of the implements were worn out and should have been junked, but Dad was unable to get his money from Gene Collins. It was a loss of ten thousand dollars, which prohibited the purchase of new machinery. Most of the farm implements of the time were simple and we could make necessary repairs with a set of end wrenches, a couple of monkey wrenches, and two or three pipe (Stillson) wrenches. Of course, the ubiquitous screwdrivers and pliers wore holes in Dad's overall pockets because he carried them nearly all the time.

There were blacksmithing tools brought from Texas, including a forge, a good anvil, and two "screw jacks" (also "jack screws"). I still have and use the anvil and the jacks. I don't know what happened to the forge, but I have replaced it with one like it. I seldom use it, but occasionally make something just for fun and it comes in handy.

One of my fond memories is of watching Dad working at the forge and anvil. He could fit horse shoes or weld a broken piece of machinery as if he did it every day. I have tried to forge weld, but there is something lacking. My welds never hold. Dad said I was a "cold iron" blacksmith.

One of the tools we brought to Illinois was a wagon tire shrinker. In the southwest, the air was very dry, the wood of the fellows would dry and shrink, and the steel rim could fall off, making it necessary either to soak the wood with water or to shrink the steel rim. It was a good trick, but Dad and Lee were good at it. Our Illinois climate was more humid and the steel rims stayed on the wheel pretty well.

We then had no use for a tire shrinker, and it lay around our shop for several years. One year, approaching the Christmas season, Lee and I found ourselves without adequate funds for presents. In desperation, we collected every available piece of scrap iron in the place, including the tire shrinker, hauled it to town, and sold it to a junk dealer.

I didn't need a tire shrinker; few retired teachers do, but I wish that I had that old tool back again. Thanks for the memories.

We were short on furniture, but Dad and Lee solved that problem by going to farm sales and used furniture stores to buy the things that we needed.

I remember well the couch that they bought. It was green, with one end elevated so you were not laying flat, and I remember thinking that it was the ugliest thing that I had ever seen. I think Mom thought so, too, but it was better than nothing. I eventually got up nerve enough to try it and found that it was very comfortable.

Grandma had taken her kitchen utensils to Lincoln. There were no cabinets in the kitchen and no counter work space, but there was a small room off the end of the kitchen which had shelves floor to ceiling, and housed the cream separator. The shelves were loaded with useful kitchen gear and supplies, from cured ham to rifle and shotgun shells.

It is impossible to cook without some kind of work space, so Dad built a nice kitchen table—not too high—as Mom was very short. The table was placed by the east kitchen window so you had a view of the garden. We frequently ate breakfast there to avoid carrying food to the dining room.

Of course, families have to eat. We had no garden produce to fall back on that first winter, but we had good stores in Lincoln and enough money to live well. We had plenty of pork and chickens, but for the first time in years, no beef of our own. We had to buy it.

In spite of having a new place to live and meeting grandparents for the first time, I got sick . . . *real* sick. Sick enough that Dad had to call a doctor, a sort of last resort in those days. It was late winter and the roads were just a series of frozen ruts, nearly impassable for cars and the temperature was below freezing even during the day.

Finally, the doctor arrived, via horse and buggy, and pronounced the malady as diphtheria. He gave me a shot of what he called toxin-antitoxin, hung big red QUARANTINE signs on all the doors, charged Dad two dollars, and went back to Lincoln.

The doctor was Ben Bradburn. He was a wonderful man and a very competent physician and surgeon. It was my privilege years later to be a good friend of his son and to have his grandsons in the school where I taught, although I never had them in my class. Needless to say, I survived the several doses of castor oil, which went along with the "toxin-antitoxin." That was Dr. Bradburn's standard treatment.

We were still under quarantine when we butchered that year. The old green couch was pulled up in front of a south window of the living room so that I could look out at the butchering and still be out of the way.

I remember seeing the big black kettles steaming as the water in them got boiling hot, ready for the scalding. I couldn't see the hogs being shot and bled, but I knew that they had been.

The dead hogs (we usually butchered four or five) were loaded on a sled and brought to the scalding area, which was nearer to the house, just outside of our yard. It was much more convenient for cutting up the carcasses, which was done in our farm shop where we had work tables and a stove for warmth.

Barrels with the open end up were leaned against the sled, and the scalding water poured into the open end. A hook was stuck in the hog's mouth, it was pushed into the barrel of hot water and sloshed around long enough for the hot water to loosen the hair. When the hog was pulled from the barrel, the men used specially shaped scrapers to remove the hair from the skin.

When all of the hair had been removed, the hog was dressed and quartered, then taken to the shop to be cut into shoulders, sides, and sausage pieces to be cured. Other parts, especially liver, heart and odd pieces of meat-like trimmings were ground into sausage or eaten fresh.

Neighbors that helped were all given fresh meat to take home, as the clean-up began. Hams and shoulders had to be cured and sometimes smoked, sausage ground, casings cleaned and stuffed and lard rendered.

It was all very fascinating. I had a chance to see the neighbor men as they went about their various jobs, each man doing his share of work, usually at the job at which he was the most adept.

Years later, I realized that this was a routine that had been developed among the group over many years, and that it was apparent, not only at the butchering, but at threshing, hay-making and other community activities as well.

I didn't know any of the neighbors, but one came to the window by the green couch, tapped on the glass, and smiled and waved at me. That made me feel that I had a good, new friend. Indeed, I did have. His name was Ed Schroeder, a young man who lived just across a couple of fields. From then on, he was one of my favorite people. Perhaps, Illinois was not going to be so bad, after all.

We were pretty proud of our new Dodge touring car, and I guess Dad and Mom wanted to take a trip before it was worn out. Cars in rural areas at that time didn't last long.

Dad had wanted to see his uncle Ed Jackson, who lived in or near Washington, Iowa. There were several children and grandchildren whom my folks had not seen for several years . . . if they ever had.

Our car was equipped with detachable side curtains for use in rainy or very cold weather. No one that we knew had a "closed-in" car and we had to look at the scenery, if any, through isinglass windows. If you don't know any better, it is fairly easy to be content with what you have. I am sure that we had a set of tire chains with us, too, but I don't think we used them on this trip. The car did not have a trunk, so extra clothing had to be carried in bags. Bags took up less room than suitcases and could be tucked into odd corners. There was only Frances and me in the back seat, and Dad and Mom in the front.

The road in front of our house had never been graveled, was a good, black muck, and was as slick as grease when it rained. We hoped to strike a graveled road soon, but were disappointed. Many of the roads that we drove over that morning were not only just plain dirt, but had been recently drug or graded and they were as slick as grease.

Surely enough, we hadn't been on the way very long before it started to rain. We stopped and put the side curtains on, and started to determine how long until dinnertime. Dinner was our noon meal on the farm. In the evening, we had supper.

I do not remember whether we had any noon meal or not. I feel sure that we did, because Mom would see that everyone was fed, whether in school or not.

We stayed that night at a little place named Bureau. I cannot find Bureau on my Illinois road map now, but someone along the way had a cabin where we could spend the night. The word motel was not a part of our vocabulary. There were no such things, just cabins. The going rate was $1.50 per night.

The next morning we looked for, and finally found, Bureau Junction. We knew when we found it because the route that we wanted was marked. There were various routes, indicated by painting different colored bands around the telephone poles, usually three colors. I don't remember which color combination our route had, but whatever it was, it led us across the Mississippi River and into Iowa. We reached Washington, and Uncle Ed's family, that night.

I don't remember very much about the people we met, only that I liked them fine, but there was not another seven or eight-year-old in the bunch.

Two cousins, Myrtle and Marcella, were operators for the telephone company, and took Frances and I, and I think some others, to see them at work. They were pushing and pulling little plugs into and out of sockets to make connections. I didn't realize for many years how important their jobs were.

My First Job

In the south, the corn being "knee high by the fourth of July" was the dream of every prairie farmer, at least in our part of the world.

We had planted our corn in rows, with the seeds planted exactly the same distance apart that the rows were and precisely opposite the seeds in the next row, thus making rows both vertically and horizontally. When the corn was a few inches high, the corn could be cultivated the long way, to plough out the weeds, then cultivated horizontally to plough out weeds in the row. After the corn was tall enough to shade the ground to curtail weeds from growing, the field was "laid by" or cultivated once more, going the long way again.

Most farmers had the Fourth of July as a goal to finish the corn and begin the harvest of the small grains like wheat and oats.

The most memorable Fourth of July for me caught us not only with the corn laid by, but with a twenty acre field of wheat cut, but not shocked. The weather had changed for the worse. Clouds were building up in the west, and the forecast was for rain.

Since the bundles had to be shocked so that the seed heads were off the ground and would be spoiled if unable to be kept dry, there was no alternative but to shuck the wheat. Lee and I worked as fast as we could, but the sun set, it got dark, and the fireworks display that we wanted to see had to be for someone else. We finished shocking the wheat. The darn clouds didn't produce enough rain to wet the bundles. I was disappointed because I had never seen fireworks.

Our visits to places of entertainment were far and few between. That was probably not without its compensations, because if familiarity breeds contempt, then perhaps, rarity breeds appreciation. Attendance at a good movie, for instance, might be spoken about for days because we saw so few.

One time, Mom and the girls took me with them when they went to a carnival. It would be a rare event now for a carnival to be operating in the afternoon, but this one was, so it could be attended without interfering with chores or farm work that had to be done evenings.

I would have liked to throw a baseball at the bottles to try for a cupie doll. I didn't want the doll, but I thought that would be the only thing that I could do to try to win something.

I didn't get to throw the ball, but we did get to buy a hot dog and a bottle of soda pop. It was orange, too.

Sister Frances was the most enthusiastic person about carnivals that I have ever known except for her daughter, Marcie. It was largely through Frances' effort that I got to ride the merry-go-round, our name for a carousel. It was a real thrill, and to this day, I like to listen to carousel music. I might even take a turn on one of the horses.

The most talked-about event of the day happened on the midway. As we were walking along through the crowd to see more of the sights, one of the carnival people had several helium-filled balloons on strings, and was walking near to us.

A stiff breeze blew the balloons toward us and one of them made contact with the point of a hat-pin which Mom was using to help hold her hat on her head. The loud "pop" caused a lot of attention to be focused on Mom, and hilarious laughter at the carnival man, who made several disparaging remarks about hats in general, and women's hats in particular.

For about a minute, it was the best sideshow on the midway.

I don't know the meaning of the word Chautaqua, but I don't feel too badly about it. After consulting two respected dictionaries, I came to the conclusion that they didn't know either.

However, I do know what some of them were like in the 1920s when my folks would attend one or more of the nightly, or sometimes afternoon, programs.

The Methodist Church was somehow involved in its organization. It made its first appearance in 1874, at Lake Chautauqua, New York. I don't know whether the lake gave its name to Chautauqua, or whether Chautauqua gave its name to the lake. I think that all the people involved in the nomenclature are dead. Anyway, if the Methodists were involved, you can bet it had something to do with religious revival and was probably done in good taste from a cultural standpoint. That, of course, is just my carefully biased opinion.

The movement was very successful, and by the time I attended a program, it had spread over much of the country. I eventually became familiar with Chautauqua Grounds at Lincoln and Mackinaw Dells. This one was a riding stable and arena when I last saw it. That was the cultural aspects still effective after more than one hundred years. There is a huge pavilion in Bloomington at Miller Park, and there has to be hundreds of the old meeting places scattered over the country, perhaps some of the cottages that were used by families who came and stayed for a week or for the summer may still be in use. I hope so.

I took part in a 4H Club operetta given at Lincoln one year. There were hundreds of guests and a large chorus. That was my sole experience as a Chautauqua performer. I was in the chorus.

Spring was a busy and sometimes disheartening time. Many farmers hired young married men and provided a small "tenant" house for the family. These little homes were not castles, being only shacks in poor condition that had been built as cheaply as possible and poorly maintained.

The first of March was moving time and the beginning of the farm work year, but still, wet, muddy, and cold. The first thing to unload for people moving in was the linoleum, if they had any floor covering at all. As soon as the floor covering was down, the heating and cooking stove were set up, and fires built to get warm and cook something for dinner (lunch). Then the rest of the furniture, bedding, clothes, and other possessions were brought in and placed. This didn't take long; there was not that much to move. One box wagon was the accepted vehicle for hauling, and one wagon could hold it all.

The going wage was fifty dollars per month. In addition, the hired man was given a hog to butcher, and if the farmer had a cow or two, he was given fresh milk daily.

The contract, actually just a verbal agreement, was closely adhered to and extended through corn-husking time. In some cases, the man was paid by the bushel for corn husking, usually four cents a bushel. A few shuckers could harvest one hundred bushels in a day, making four dollars. Most men made much less than that, because the old time open-pollinated corn stalks frequently bent over and the ears were laying on the ground, perhaps even covered with snow. After corn harvest, the hired man was "laid off" without pay until the first of March. The farmer had problems, too. Annual income for many was less than four hundred dollars per year.

As soon as the last bundle of wheat or oats was in the shock, the next big job was threshing. The threshing machine is essentially a large metal or wood box mounted on four steel wheels. Most of the moving parts that actually do the work of separating the grain from the straw and chaff are inside the box. The intake part is on the front and is called the feeder. The straw is blown out the rear through a long tube called the blower. The blower can be raised or lowered, may be pointed left or right, and has an adjustable hood on the outer end which enables a good operator to build a stack of straw shaped so that it will shed water, thus keeping the straw in good condition for winter feeding or bedding for livestock.

The feeder is a flat trough, deep enough to keep the bundles from falling out, and wide enough for two bundles to lay side by side. This enables two bundle haulers to feed the machine at the same time, if desired.

The bundles are fed into the body of the machine by two endless chains, one on each side of the feeder, connected to each other by wood slats which drag the bundles to moving knives which cut the bundle strings and scatter the straw before it goes into the beaters and shakers. Eventually, the straw is blown out and the clean grain is carried to a boxlike device where it is weighed, measured, and fed through an auger-tube, leading to a wagon, truck or trailer to haul it to the farm grainery or to a grain elevator for sale.

The threshing machine, or separator, is powered by a tractor or engine with a long drive belt from the power pulley to the separator.

The threshing machine in our neighborhood was owned by Dad, Carl (Doc) Baker, and Ed Schroeder.

As soon as the wheat and oats had been shocked, the machine was brought to our house and parked under the trees which Grandpa, his father, and uncle had planted in two rows between the house and the barn. The machine was a J. I. Case, with a twenty-eight-inch-wide feeder. It was metal, and when it was in the sun, could get real *hot* to work on.

It was checked for adjustments or needed repairs, and was given whatever was needed to prevent breakdowns during the threshing seasons, when every minute counts. Lee had always been the one to crawl inside the machine to check the beaters and the shakers, and if necessary, remove them for repairs,

When I was twelve or thirteen, I was given the job. I wanted to do it, it looked like fun when I was standing under a shade tree, and Lee was in the "guts" of the machine.

Finally, Lee yielded to me, and, as usual, coached me in the intricacies of threshing machine mechanics. It was hot in there but I felt that I had a real grown-up responsibility (which it was) and I enjoyed every minute of it.

I had reached one of the goals that I had aimed for since the day that Doc Baker handed me a very heavy hammer and put me to work breaking up coal chunks for the old steam engine which we were using at that time. I was about six years old.

When I had a sizeable pile of coal for the boiler, he gave me a nickel. It was the first one I ever earned and I wish that I had kept it, but it went the way of all of the other nickels I have earned. I spent it. I am sure the angels smiled on Doc, not just for me, but for many other deeds as well.

Later, the company sold the steam engine and the old J. I. Case separator, replacing it with a new, smaller machine which they powered with their own farm tractors, each owner using his tractor every third year. However, the threshing season was never the same after we quit using the steam engine and the big separator. That old steam engine made beautiful music and if I had it, I would fire it up and just sit and listen to it; perhaps blowing the whistle once in a while.

My first real job was hauling the grain from the threshing machine to the elevator. Bell Station, the elevator eventually to become the West Lincoln Farmers Grain Company, was owned and operated by the farmers in West Lincoln Township.

We hauled the grain in farm wagons, pulled by a team of horses. It was about four miles, round trip, to the elevator and we would make the trip three or four times a day from our farm. No one in our run had a truck, but traffic was not a problem. If a car met or passed us, they would drive slowly, but no one expected to see more than three or four cars in a day. Everyone was at work.

The wagons held about fifty bushels of wheat, unless you added extra sideboards, and at our place, we usually had four or five wagons hauling so the machine didn't have to stop and wait for haulers.

When we got to the elevator, we sometimes had to wait in line for the wagons from other neighborhoods to empty. When our turn came, we drove up a long ramp to a level upper floor, and stopped with the wheels in a shallow depression or blocked to keep the wagon from rolling back. This position had the back of the wagon directly over a covered chute.

There were two large ropes hanging from above, one on each side of the front wheels. Each rope had a loop at the lower end which fit over the hub of the wheel. After these were fastened, the cover over the chute was raised, the rear endgate opened, the grain rolled out into the chute, a lever was pulled and the ropes raised the front end of the wagon so that it could be completely emptied.

Power for the lift was furnished by a huge one-cylinder, semi-diesel stationary engine.

Riding on a wagon behind a team of good, well-educated horses is the best place in the world to do some thinking. The crunch of the steel-rimmed wheels on the gravel furnished the background music for us (the horses and me) and we wanted for nothing except one of the (still a little bit green) apples from Harold Fue's good orchard, which bordered the road.

When I was fifteen, we had a shortage of competent farm workers. It was 1931, one of the worst of the Great Depression years, and there were dozens of unemployed workers in our county.

In early July, we had grain harvested, but still laying on the ground, needing to be shocked, and the forecast was for rain. Lee went to town to see if he could hire one or two men to shock the oats. The city park had several unemployed men sitting on the benches, so Lee asked if there was anyone who would like a job shocking oats.

The answer that he got, along with ribald laughter was, "Are they tame or wild oats?" No one was willing to do that kind of work.

Lee came home empty-handed and we worked well into the night getting the seed heads off the ground.

That was the year that I tried to convince Dad that I could run a basket rack and haul bundles to the threshing machine. Dad thought I was too young, but I finally got his consent. I knew that it would save hiring a man, even if one was available. The wage at that time was three dollars a day, and I knew that we needed to save every dollar that we could. I stuck it out, but I wished before it was over that I had been a couple of years older and fifty pounds heavier.

There was one incident that I do have cause to remember. Carl Baker's son, Harold (young Doc) was, like me, hauling bundles for the first time. We also had a hired man on the job who was large and strong. His name was Claude Workman and one day, he complained that "them kids" were not hauling their share of the bundles. Doc and I had been hauling about thirty shocks per load, which is three hundred thirty bundles to load, and three hundred thirty to throw into the feeder.

When we heard about the complaint, we decided to haul in more than he did. We loaded forty-one shocks and headed for the machine. So far, so good. On the way to the machine, we had to cross a shallow swale which put an extra load on the coupling pole that connects the front axle to the rear one, snapping it in two and leaving my rack setting there in the field with over four hundred bundles which had to be loaded on another rack to get them to the machine. Need I say more? Believe me, I went back to hauling my thirty shock loads.

Dad, who was running the separator, never said a word. I found an oak two-by-four fourteen feet long, fitted it to the axels, and I never said a word, either.

The threshing days are gone now, except for a few instances where people are hanging onto the memories.

I wish that I could have an old separator now to look at occasionally and to show young people, even though there have been times when I wished that I had never seen one.

There are thresher-mens reunions held in some places, and I hope they continue to hold their exhibitions for the good of their communities. The great combines that are used today are worthy descendents. The people of the world must be fed.

Country School

Finally, the day came when I had to go to school. It is probably a good thing that I do not remember much about the warnings that I had about behavior, like that I should always call the teacher "Miss" before saying her name, keep my shoes clean, and so on. Sister Frances did most of the prep work and I guess I felt like I could handle it. At least, I don't remember *dreading* it.

The school in our township was called West Point, presumably because it was in West Lincoln Township. In later years, I could tell people that I was a graduate of West Point. Some of them seemed a little bit surprised until I told them *which* West Point.

Originally, the school was only one room, built on a plot of land donated by the Liesman family. Soon after we moved to Illinois, but before I started to school, a "cloak room" was built across the front. It had benches built against the wall at each end; one end for girls, one end for boys. All of us walked to school, except in the worst weather, so we all had overshoes to take off and on, making those benches a real treat.

They also had a room built across the back of the schoolroom. It was for the coal that we burned in the big furnace and the corn cobs that we used in place of kindling wood to start the fire.

During the coldest part of the winter, it was a real challenge to get the fire started early enough to warm the room before school "took up."

Some of the new teachers were town girls, just out of college. They had never tried to start a fire and had a hard time of it. If they were lucky, there would be one or more seventh or eighth grade boys to carry the coal and cobs and light and tend the fire.

After school was dismissed at the end of the day, the fire was "banked," so that there would be at least a few hot coals to start the fire the next morning. Overnight, the building would cool off enough to be uncomfortable, and if very cold, we would move our desks closer to the furnace and hold our feet up farther from the cold floor.

Maintenance and any new construction was done by members of the school board, consisting of three "directors," or by someone hired by them. The carpentry work done on our building was as fine as you could find any place, and this was at a time when such work was done by hand by Carl Baker, Reynold Liesman, Joe Katz, Frank Baker, Henry Paulus, and/or Dad (the *other* Harry Jackson).

The building was located several feet from the road and about the middle of the school yard. I believe there was an acre or more for a really nice playground. On the west, there were several large trees which made excellent bases for our games like dare base and capture the flag. They also provided dead leaves, twigs, and limbs for the traditional leaf house that we built every fall. The boys usually built the leaf house while the girls stayed inside with the teacher or played some of their own games.

The leaf house was snug and warm and large enough for all of the boys to eat their lunches there. The east side of the playground was all cleared of brush and trees, except for two beautiful sugar maples that grew next to the road. This area was the greatest for the running games that we played and for baseball.

The game we played the most we called Blackman. I have heard it called dare base, Ace, and there are probably other names for it. It consisted of two bases, which were parallel lines between two objects and about fifty feet apart. One player was "it" or "Ace," who ranged between the two bases while the other players, called runners, tried to reach the other base without being tagged. If you were tagged, you had to assist "it" to try to tag the others. The term Blackman had no reference at all to the negro race. The thought never occurred to us that it might be derogatory. I doubt any children today even play this wonderful game, and if so, they would have to call it by a different name, such as Ace.

Harold Katz's father made us a ball bat. Sometimes, we used a sponge rubber ball because you could get them at a Kresge or Woolworth five-and-ten-cent store. You could buy baseballs there, too, but they didn't last long. The covers came off after the first or second game, then we would wrap the ball with black rubber tape and get several more recess games out of it.

I never knew a piece of sporting goods or game equipment to be furnished to West Point by the directors. I guess their taxes were high enough that they didn't want to add more costs.

Now, schools are required to provide Health and Physical Education time in class. In schools of large enrollments of today, that is a fine thing, and competition in sports has great value, but I wish these poor little kids could play just one game of Blackman.

Harry and Mildred

I have tried to paint word pictures of our life and times, and I find that, in some instances, it is difficult to do without painting, at least in part, some of the background.

I must have been about eight or nine years old, when the directors hired a new teacher. Her name was Albina Nailin. I am not certain of the spelling, but I am of the pronunciation. She was a fine young woman from Lincoln, and this was her first teaching position. She probably had never been on a farm in her life, and to be thrown into the mud roads, building fires in the school furnace, and a group of semi-literate kids was very trying for her. Of course, we pupils didn't know how to help her, and probably wouldn't have if we had known. In our primative childhood society, it was "each for himself," and "saddle your own horse" attitude. We had grown up with it and didn't know any different.

It was not long before she began to see the light, and to let us know that she had. One of the most vivid of my recollections was of Miss Nailin deciding that we needed something hot for our lunch. There were only eight or nine of us, so it shouldn't have been a big deal. How to make soup? No one claimed to know. Who could find out? I raised my hand (I was confident that my mom and/or sisters would know). If not, I suspected that a little girl named Mildred Baker would.

Mildred was the daughter of Ed and Amelia Baker, who lived a half mile north of us. "Aunt Meal" was a kind of second mother to me, so since Mildred and I walked the first quarter mile toward home, we determined that I would stop at her house and see what her mother thought. Incidentally, this was the usual procedure for most of our plans.

Well, it worked out fine. I brought a quart of home-canned tomatoes and Mildred brought a quart of milk. The community club had a two-burner kerosene stove and plenty of cups.

Mildred was in the third grade and the oldest girl, so she was elected to make the soup. It was great. Every family took their turn at supplying the milk and tomatoes, so we had soup every day for lunch until the warmer days of spring.

Mildred and I were playmates and there were very few days in the summer when we did not have some kind of project to plan. She had a little black pony named Bobby. We would hitch Bobby to her cart and carry fresh water to the men in the field when we were thrashing or putting up hay.

Her grandfather, Uncle Nick, was retired and living with Ed and Meal. If he overheard us say we wanted something, you could bet that we would soon have it. One stormy day in winter, Mildred and I were on the floor, looking through a Montgomery Ward catalogue. We were studying what it said about a "Baker" tent. "Just right for children campers," the catalogue claimed. How we wished we had one!

Sure enough, a few days later, Aunt Meal called Mom, and asked if I could come down right away and asked that I please hurry. When I arrived, on the living room floor was a huge bundle of "Baker" tent.

We were twelve or thirteen when the Bakers moved to Michigan. Mildred came home with her mother on a visit to her relatives and came out to the field where I was working. It was difficult to communicate. We were complete strangers but I will never forget her and the tomato soup.

The personal relationships between my schoolmates were, for the most part, peaceful and enjoyable. Most of the games that we played at recess were simple activities without complicated rules, requiring an umpire or a coach and were as much fun for the girls as for the boys. While the rules were simple, they were as sacred as the Ten Commandments and no one ever knowingly violated them. To do so would be sufficient cause to bar you from all games, and that never happened. It was just an unwritten code of behavior handed down through the entire community.

Older pupils were considerate of the younger ones, frequently faking "falling down" or making it possible in some way for the young one to catch or tag the older, larger player. If a strange "bully" would have molested or insulted one of us, they would have had the whole group to whip.

It fell to me one time to straighten out a situation that kind of "sneaked" up on us. One of the older boys was a sort of devil sometimes, and he thought it great fun to aggravate the pupil in front of him by tweaking their ear with a pencil. It just happened that on a particular day I was the pupil in front of him. I endured the tweaks until recess time when we were all out under one of the big maple trees. I told the kid that I had had enough and that there was not going to be any more of it, not only to me, but to anyone else.

He was surprised that I would stand up to him. I was a little bit surprised, too, but I was also angry. When he asked me what I was going to do about it, I must have done something.... When I again realized that something *was* going on, I was astraddle on his chest with an ear in each hand, and beating his head on an above ground tree root under that big maple. I had completely blacked out.

Our teacher at that time was a young neighborhood girl, Lucille Flick. On that particular day, Miss Flick was ill and her sister, Florence, was substituting for her. I guess my behavior upset her and she was standing there crying and not knowing what to do. The rest of the pupils were just standing there with their mouths open, too. I got up off the ground, helped my friend up (yes, he was my friend then and was for many years, until he died a few years ago) and we all went back into the school room and resumed our studies.

That was the last of the ear tweaking, at least as long as I attended West Point. Until this writing, this escapade was never mentioned again.

I was in the fourth grade when this happened. Miss Lucille later taught my son, Kenneth, when he was in the fourth grade at the Washington-Monroe School in Lincoln, and I was her principal. She was a wonderful person, a great teacher, and we all loved her. Hundreds of pupils that were in her classes will never forget her. I won't either.

The teacher was pretty busy, and I had a lot of time to sit and listen to the other pupils recite. We didn't always have all eight grades, so in addition to me, there may be only five or six other grades to listen to.

The teacher would call the pupils in a particular grade to come to the front of the room, where they could sit on a bench facing the teacher at her desk.

The teacher would open the textbook and ask questions that the children were supposed to have prepared to answer. Sometimes, the pupils could answer the questions, especially if the teachers gave them enough hints. I learned a lot about asking questions, but I didn't take much stock in the answers which the pupils gave. This went on for seven years. It would have been eight, except that I went through two grades (five and six) in one year. I was always alone in my grade, so I had enough freedom to compare students and teachers for both content and mastery. I became pretty competent at both. After all, I had the best of everything for seven years. I learned to spot the A's from the B's (and F's) pretty easily.

For example: We had a little girl pupil in the sixth grade. She was very shy, poorly dressed—her father was one of those fifty-dollars-a-month farmhands—and not too bright. She was also a new pupil that year and had not been well received by the other pupils.

Her assignment had been to study the section on Africa in her geography, and she had done so. The teacher said, "Describe the climate of Africa." The child hesitated a bit, then answered, "It's hot and dry with lots of rainfall."

Every word of her answer was true, of course, as far as it could be determined under these circumstances.

The sad part was that everyone in the room except me and the teacher laughed. I felt more like crying for that child.

In the first place, it was an impossible question to answer, short of a doctoral dissertation. I knew about what the teacher wanted, but I don't think that she did, so I mentally gave the child an A and the teacher an F.

I believe, strongly, that the sharing of one room with multiple grades was one of the advantages of the country school. One of the major problems for the teachers was that there were not enough pupils in any one grade to make valid comparisons.

It was almost impossible to have a pupil repeat a grade. Parents very rarely would admit that their son or daughter was not fully prepared for the next grade, and if they were not promoted, the teacher looked for another job. Their philosophy was pretty much, "If the pupil doesn't learn, the teacher hasn't taught." Sometimes, that is true, I am sure. It is also true that if the pupil doesn't want to learn, and actively refuses, there is no teacher that I have ever met that could accomplish much with them.

Good teachers will keep on trying.

Most of the rural school districts had Community Clubs. These were regular monthly meetings between the parents and the teacher.

The only officer in our club was the president, who called the meeting to order and sometimes led the group in singing a few songs from the old yellow song book. He then turned the meeting over to the program committee. This committee sometimes had guest performers, semi-local individuals, or prepared the program themselves.

My folks liked to be on the committee with Harold and Lynn Fue and Joe and Bertha Katz. Lee and Clarice usually prepared some musical numbers, a couple of short one-act plays. They studied the catalogues relentlessly, trying to find material that would appeal to the local audience.

They were seldom performed as written. Sometimes large portions of the script were rewritten to fit the audience, a neat trick that not everyone can do. The little stages in the schoolhouse were not designed for theatrical endeavors, but Lee could take a few boards or whatever was available and convince an audience that it was a regular Broadway production.

Frances was a good little actress and had a sweet singing voice. Dad usually wrote and presented a monologue. They were not sermons, and they were not comedy; they were just Dad. Being the kind of man that he was, they could not have been anything else. Mr. Fue could be a hilarious comedian, and Mr. Katz was the same. People that had known these two all their lives never dreamed of their latent talent. Everyone did their best, and they were great.

Most of us tried to get to school early enough that we could play a game or visit a while before classes began. Our day was well-arranged. We began with reading, which I loved, followed by English, which I hated. We had a fifteen-minute recess, and then arithmetic. I always had a problem with arithmetic, I never could develop a real interest in it. I would just do my assignment to get it over with, quickly do what I had to for spelling, history or geography, then spend the rest of the day with a good library book.

Once in a while, I would hang up on an arithmetic problem. I liked that unless it was too difficult. Sometimes, the teacher was unable to solve it, too. In that case, I took it home and Lee would take one look at it and solve it.

We had a school library. It was four feet wide, and five shelves high. We only could buy one or two new books each year. I had read every book we had by the time I was finished with the third grade. So I read them again. I can still quote from some of them.

This was the time I started reading Zane Grey. He wrote several books for young people, but not for fourth and fifth graders. I read them anyway, when I found one that I could borrow. After that, I graduated to *Wild West Weekly, Western Story Magazine* and any other works of adventure that I could find.

I never had a classmate. I guess I was glad because I had a lot more freedom, but that didn't make it any easier for me when I started high school.

I worked at home all of that summer, except for one week. Harold Fue was an active participant in the Farm Bureau, and needed to be gone from home for a few days. I agreed to help him, moved over (only a mile) to his house because I did all of the chores, fed and harnessed the horses and ate breakfast before going to the neighbors, where we were threshing that day.

It was a small run, the only farmers that I can remember were Frank Flick, Frank Kiest, and George Oltman. I am sure that there were others, but I probably didn't even know at the time who they were.

I was hauling bundles to the machine, but didn't have to work too hard. I had time to make a few adjustments on the grain-measuring apparatus so the men had a better idea of the number of bushels threshed. Apparently, no one knew that the machine could be made to measure the grain accurately, related to the moisture content, but perhaps they didn't care for that degree of accuracy.

The machine was a Keck-Gonnerman. It was a really sweet-running machine, and I really enjoyed that week. I must also give a great deal of credit to Mrs. Fue (Lynn) who, knowing how much I liked apple salad, made sure that I had all I could eat of it. The Fues were among the dearest of our neighbors and friends.

The teen years are generally recognized as being the age when many of the basic beliefs and behavior patterns are developed. These "formative years" are that time when the young person feels like a competent adult one minute and a disoriented fish-out-of-water kid the next.

My life had been so regulated by parents and siblings (as it should be), by the accepted customs of the locality, weather, and economics, that I remember feeling that I was engulfed by factors beyond my control. I think that I was unconsciously looking for something to do that was different and that was of my own making. I had given little or no thought to a possible vocation. In a middle-western farm community, your choices were limited at best, and many, if not most, farm boys were expected to follow in their father's footsteps. However, circumstances alter cases, and in my case, the circumstance was the Great Depression, a love for reading, and a release from boredom.

During my one-room school days, I had read and reread a book entitled *Tom Slade, Motorcycle Dispatch Bearer*. It was the story of a young man (Tom) and his adventures in France while carrying messages for the U.S. Army during World War I.

It seems that Tom had been a boy scout and the training and the adventures that he had in scouting were standing him in good stead while doing his very important work for the army. This book was the first challenge. Although I had known for a long time that there were such things as boy scouts, the only thing that I associated with them was that they went on hikes. Whatever for, I didn't know.

I found a few other books that told of scouting adventures and enjoyed all of them but never gave a thought to ever joining a troop. Boy Scout troops were always associated, in my mind, with boys who lived in town, so that eliminated them from my plans. We lived too far from our town for me to participate.

Eventually my country school days came to an end and in the Spring, I had to go to Lincoln to take the county final examination. This was my first and only opportunity to see and meet all of the young people who would, hopefully, be my classmates when we entered high school in the Fall. I didn't realize at the time that there were members of a sizeable minority who, for one reason or another, would not plan to enter high school at all and that their formal education was completed.

We were all gathered for the exam in the large main study hall at Lincoln Community High School. The examination was administered by the county superintendent, Mr. E. H. Lukenbill. He was well-known to all of the pupils, as he visited each of the county schools twice a year. He visited with the pupils and if conditions were favorable, would join us at recess for part of a ball game. I thought that he was really a special person because on one visit to our school, he had a rather long conference with our teacher, Miss Bessie Martinie. I remember some of us hoping that he might make the school board buy us a new bat and ball. Later, I found out what the confab was about. He recommended that I be allowed to complete both the fifth and the sixth grade in one year, a situation that pleased both Miss Martinie and me. Miss Martinie later became my much loved sister-in-law. The only thing I didn't like was that she took my brother away from me!

After the noon break and before we resumed the remaining tests, Mr. Lukenbill introduced a young man who had been standing nearby. He was Mr. Donald E. Kyger, the boy scout executive for the Logan County Council Of the Boy Scouts, and he was given a few minutes to explain a new program in scouting especially designed for boys who could not attend regular troop meetings. It required only an adult advisor to assist the scout with his training, test his knowledge of the requirements for advancement and help with the merit badge program, as needed. The Lone Scout, as they were called, would be welcome to visit any established troop and would be considered a brother scout.

If we desired any further information, we could come to the scout office in the City Hall building after the exams were completed.

I went.

As I look back on this day I realize how important it was to me. My life was changed to the extent that I had a glimmer of hope for a future different from what I had thought it might be. There were possibilities in the world that I did not know about, but I knew that it was likely that I would find out. I was ready to give it a try.

I had paid my fifty cents for membership and agreed that as soon as I could raise a dollar and a half more, I could get the *Boy Scout Handbook For Boys*. In the meantime, Mr. Kyger loaned me one of his. Fortunately, Dad had enough money to go back and get my own copy. I still have it. It is in a place of honor in one of my book cases, and I consider it a treasure.

I had always been something of a loner, but I felt the need for the first time to have someone share my good fortune. There were three boys of scouting age in the Martinie family that attended the same little country church that we did. They were my former teacher's brothers: Charles, Donald, and Dick. They were great fun to be with and we soon organized as a lone scout patrol. I was the first lone scout in Logan County and our patrol was the first in the county. My brother was our advisor.

About this time, it became known in our neighborhood that Rear Admiral Richard E. Byrd intended to take an eagle scout on his trip of discovery to the South Pole. I started to work immediately on the requirements for eagle rank, only to find out that I was too late and that the article that I had read failed to mention the fact that the applicant must have a Ph.D. degree or the equivalent. I was extremely unhappy about it . . . for about a week.

I never got to go to a summer scout camp. The camp session always came at the busiest time of the year for farm people, and my folks could not afford to hire a man to replace me.

I never got scouting out of my mind and in later years made up for anything that I had missed as a young scout. Over the years, I served for fifteen years as a scoutmaster, and held many other positions of responsibility in the local council. I never was a den mother, but my wife was and I deserve some credit for that!

In 1953, I was awarded the *Silver Beaver,* which is limited to highly select volunteers in each council. It is the highest award given to an adult in scouting, and I treasure it.

I do have some regrets: for many years I spent so much time scouting that I neglected my own wife and son, and I wish now that I had cut back a little on the service that I felt I needed to render.

High School

The summer of 1930 was drawing to a close. About the third week of August, I received a letter from Mr. W. C. Handlin, the principal of the high school, giving the information needed for the coming term. All freshmen (already I hated that word) would report on the opening day and "would need the following supplies." Supplies, of course, included text books, a "gym suit," and all of the other things that go with the first day of school in most places. Also included was the program of classes, the assignment to a "session" room, and the room numbers of the various classes.

I was the first member of my family to attend high school, so we were a little bit puzzled be the term "session" room. We finally deduced that it was the place to go in the morning, and again after lunch, for the roll to be taken, announcements made and a "home" room teacher to get you out of trouble if the trouble wasn't too great.

Finally, the great day came. My home room teacher was Miss Yvonne Koehnle, and was pretty much just what the doctor ordered to put us at ease and make us really feel at home, or at least, as much as possible.

There were about thirty pupils in the room, and that was a situation that I had never faced before. Fortunately, there were three or four boys that I knew and that were just as scared as I was. We were branded "farmers" right off, but it was just a means of distinguishing us from the larger group, which consisted of pupils who came from junior high in Lincoln.

At the sound of the bell, we scattered to our various classes. I have long ago forgotten the order in which the classes came, but vividly remember the courses and the teachers that I had.

My first class, and the scariest, was English, a subject that I would have liked to have lived without. I soon found myself so lost that I couldn't believe that I had ever spoken the language. I was not alone. Our teacher (a very pretty young lady) was new at teaching and I think that she tried to impress the class. It took a while, but finally I learned enough of the "lingo" to know what was going on. Here is an example: The teacher wrote a sentence on the chalk board and asked me to underline all of the nominatives. I had never heard the word "nominative" before. So, that is what I told her. All the kids laughed (a sure way to get me good and mad). The teacher threw up her hands very dramatically. I sat down.

The teacher asked another kid who went through the sentence underlining such words as "chair," "book," and so on. Suddenly I burst out with, "Oh, you mean *nouns.*"

Pretty or not, she never got to be one of my favorite teachers. One other incident almost put a cap on our association. We were asked to write a short story, telling of an experience that we had supposedly had. It could be truth or fiction. I decided to write a true one.

I worked diligently on my story, sitting at one end of our big dining table while Dad and Mom, and my sisters, Clarice and Frances, played cards on the other half.

My story dealt with an event that happened when I was about eight or nine years old. Actually, I was more like twelve or thirteen. I had gone down the road a half mile to spend a few hours with my brother, Lee and his wife, Bessie. Our wind mill was near the barn and except for the gears, was made of wood. It hardly made a sound when it was in gear and was pumping water. However, in order to have a story, I had it of steel and very noisy. Well, in the story I was walking home, heard the screeching of the windmill, thought it might be a wild animal or a ghost (I didn't remember which) got scared, ran home, only to find that it was the windmill as I passed it on the way to the house. I dolled up the "getting scared" part pretty good, and put a nice glad-to-be-home ending on it. The next day, I handed it in just like the others did.

It came back with an "F." Also written across the page was, "What did you copy this from?"

Of course, everyone in the class knew about it. I never denied it.

I took it home, showed it to Dad, and waited for the ax to fall. He wrote a courteous note to the teacher, explaining how and when it had been written and put it in an envelope addressed to her. I gave it to her, but nothing was ever said about it. I got a B grade for the semester and knew I was lucky. It was a long time before I would trust an English teacher and it was many years before I told the principal about it. At the time I told him, we were discussing "old times" and I was teaching in the junior high school in Lincoln.

My algebra class was a real joy after English. The teacher was a fine-looking young man named Jack Hodgson. He called the roll and made jokes with some of the pupils who he seemed to know. For those who were strangers to him, he asked about where we lived, how our folks got along, or anything else that he could think of to get us over being afraid of algebra, just to be helpful. He had met with nervous freshmen before.

I didn't know, or even suspect, that we would ever be closely associated in any way, but I spent many hours in his classes in mechanical drawing and architecture and the friendship continued for many years after high-school graduation. He was also the main track coach and he was pleased to know that I could run the cross-country two miles in just a few seconds over twelve minutes. Unfortunately, I could not compete in track because I had to catch my ride to and from school and was confined to activities within the school-day hours.

In our school system, the academic program was designed especially to fit the needs of the pupils. Consequently, shop and agriculture (both double-time classes) could both be taken in place of Latin, which was a required course for college prep students. There was one drawback—there was not time for the number of study hall hours desirable for the academic subjects, therefore, more homework. All pupils were also excused from general science and biology. I was disappointed when I found that I would have to miss biology, as I wanted the knowledge and also to take a course taught by Mr. Lara Hardin, a fine man and a great teacher.

My agricultural teacher was Mr. Ralph Morray, who for the first time, made us proud to be students of the land and its products. He told us we were as respectable and intelligent as the "city slickers," although he didn't use those words.

The first year dealt with soils and crops, the second year we studied animal husbandry.

I had looked forward to "manual training," which, for the first year, was woodwork, branching eventually into building trades. Most of the building trade instruction was introduced into the curriculum after I had graduated. I still built two houses (with my wife's help) based largely on skills I had learned and developed in the wood shop.

The instructor, Walter Alde, was at least the equal of any teacher that I ever had as a craftsman, as a model teacher and as a gentleman. Every student whom he ever taught was a better person because of the association.

Every member of my family was a musician . . . except me. For fourteen years, all that I had done was listen to the music that the others made. That was about to change. Lincoln Community High School had two bands, the regular band that played at the football games, and other special events, and a beginner's band that never really played, just made a heck of a racket up in the bandroom, which was in the attic.

I couldn't afford an instrument (remember that we were in the very worst years of the Great Depression) and, as well, I didn't feel that I had the time to grow proficient on a wind instrument.

One day, I saw a note on the bulletin board. FOR SALE: DRUM. TEN DOLLARS. SEE THE BAND DIRECTOR.

I went to see the band director, Professor H. O. Merry, a really great gentleman. He said, "Harry, the drum is worth at least fifty dollars, but if you will learn to play well enough to play in the regular band, you can have it for ten, and pay me when you can. We need another drummer."

I went to beginners' band for two weeks, then to the regular band. They played a lot of Sousa marches and I handled it pretty well. I played in the band all four years and got a music letter. I also paid the ten dollars. I don't know where Dad dug up that much money, but he didn't want me to have to accept charity of any form.

Our band uniforms consisted of a red and green cape and little hat. We furnished our own white pants. Football games can get pretty chilly with a rig like that, but I was proud to be one of the gang.

I wanted, in the worst way, to be in the boys' glee club. The teacher to see about that was George Arthur Browne. We had tryouts to see what parts fit our voices, and I was accepted as second tenor. I really enjoyed the songs that Mr. Browne selected for us, the *Winter Song, Rolling Down to Rio,* and others. Most important of all, was getting to know Mr. Browne. He was the Dean of Boys, taught Physics (which I didn't have until my senior year), and in my sophomore year, selected eight of us to be a double quartet. We met after school and sang spirituals and many of the old male quartet favorites. After we had adjusted to each other, we performed at the Rotary and Kiwanis clubs, and for several other groups in Lincoln.

The only real problem that I had with the singing groups was identified and largely corrected by the lady music teacher, Miss Helmi Lahti, who was also a very fine singer in her own right. She said my voice was very weak, so she put me in a small group that she considered worthy of special attention, and put us to work on voice placement and control. She saw to it that we did our own work, too. I learned a lot about what to do to make singing easier and a real joy.

It was no secret among the music students that she and my shop teacher, Mr. Walter Alde, were very much in love, and we all hoped they would do something about it.

They did.

Unfortunately, that was the end of our association with Helmi Lahti Alde, and we all missed her very much.

There were good sides, too, about that. The vacancy was filled by another very wonderful teacher, Miss Frances Mantle. She helped me a great deal during the next three years, and finally directed all of the group singing (except the double quartet).

It seemed as if the "double quartet" was here to stay, and I guess it did hang on longer than most impromptu organizations, but eventually, some of the fellows began to lose interest, or at least as much interest as the rest of us had. To a couple of us, it seemed that we could do more, so we discussed the situation and decided to keep up with our regular weekly get-together, but asked Mr. Browne if he would care if four of us started out on our own.

Mr. Browne was enthused about it, so four of us tried it.

We met one evening at Wayne's parents' house, and after a few bars, we began to get the feel of each others' voices, and we liked it. We sang, as usual, without accompaniment (a capella) and could sense that there was something that was not quite right. It was several days of practice later that we suddenly became aware of the fact that, for the first time, we were singing *together*, each one listening to the other three.

We practiced as much as we could spare time for, called ourselves the Harmony-Four, and continued to sing together all through high school. One of the things that we enjoyed the most was going to country school community clubs to entertain the club members. They fed well, but only rarely were we reimbursed for travel expenses. I will say more about the Harmony-Four later.

My Four-H Club work was not so successful. I had bought a real nice Duroc Jersey gilt, hoping to win some prize money at the fair and to produce some world-famous stock. The gilt was to be registered by the seller, so he asked me what name we should give her. I knew nothing about proper naming of registered stock, so I suggested the name "Doris," after the most loved light-of-my-life girl in the whole world, my six-month-old niece, the daughter of my brother Lee and his wife, Bessie. *That* Doris was never a disappointment to me.

The red Duroc was, but it wasn't her fault. She had only four little piglets, healthy enough, but severely lacking in quality. At the Christian County Fair, the pen of pigs didn't even win a ribbon, but their mother got second place in the breeding sow class for all breeds.

I went out of the pig business.

The last major topic for study in our agriculture class was animal husbandry. It dealt with the different breeds of stock, their origins, strengths and weaknesses, breeding, genetics, and other related factors. It was an interesting time for me, especially regarding "hands-on" experiences that were part of the study of body conformation. Breeders were changing from producing short, low, overfed stock, to taller, longer, more rangy form in both fat cattle and hogs. Some of the older farmers did not favor the later trends, but gradually changed their minds when they heard of the animals produced by the 4H-club members bringing better prices at the stockyards.

By taking field trips to some of the local stockfarms and visiting the homes of the students with livestock-related 4H club projects, we became familiar with those characteristics that made one animal of a breed better or worse than another and to look for traits that were desirable or undesirable in breeding stock.

From the students in the class, Mr. Morray selected teams of four boys, each to represent Lincoln Community High School in the State Livestock Judging Contest. There would be one team for each category of stock: Horses, Dairy Cows, Poultry, and Fat Stock (farm horses, hogs, fat cattle and sheep).

The contest was to be held at Stonington, and I was assigned to the fat stock team.

I felt fairly secure in rating the horses, beef cattle, and hogs. We did not have sheep on our farm, and all I knew about them was what I had learned in Agriculture class. I was doubtful about my ability to judge them correctly.

Eventually we were called to the section where the stock was penned or tied and we were on our own.

I don't know how many schools participated, but it was a state contest and it seemed to me that there was an awfully big crowd.

Eventually, the judging was completed and we had to wait for some time for the results to be announced. They started with the dairy stock, then the poultry, and finally, the fat stock.

We were delighted when they announced that our school had placed third. By the time they were ready to announce the individual winners, I was about half-asleep. Finally, someone kicked me and said, "Hey, get up there!"

I came to in a hurry and made my way to the announcer. "Harry Jackson, Lincoln Community High School, Individual Judge, Second Place!"

I, a Sophomore, had done really well, and I was mighty happy . . . as were my folks.

At our next school assembly, I got to sit on the stage with some of the other big whigs on the campus, and be recognized for something besides athletics.

The Junior-Senior Banquet

It was during my Junior Year that I first began to get enthused about school. I think it was primarily due to the fact that I had really begun to live practically just to learn.

I know that I owe my sister Frances' husband, Maurice Lalicker, a great deal for a remark that he made to me one day when he first found out that I was going to high school. "Take chemistry," he said. I don't know why that remark has stayed with me all these years, but it has. I did take chemistry, and it did much to open doors for me all through the years. My teacher, Harold Luebchow, carried on where Maurice left off, and for years, I was more at home in a chem lab than any other place in the school.

I followed through by taking all of the math courses that I could have time for, missing only calculus.

It didn't hurt anything, of course, that I took four years of English (in spite of my first teacher). I even learned to thoroughly enjoy Shakespeare and to tolerate Chaucer.

The Harmony Four was still in business, having rehearsed frequently through the summer and performing in several programs.

In our school at that time, we had, in place of a prom, a Junior-Senior Banquet. It was a nice dress-up affair, many of the boys bringing their best girl, although dates were not mandatory. It was a nice affair and I enjoyed it very much. I don't think that I had a date. If I did, I don't remember it.

For many of us, it was the first exposure that we had to any cultural experience, and as far as I was concerned, it had a trip to the fast-food place beat by a mile. I think that I was beginning to wake up.

In spite of my newfound attachment to learning, I had not given up participating in the music program, expanding to the boys' chorus, the mixed chorus, an a mild shakedown try at vocal solo. The vocal solo was a washout. I sang "The Road to Mandalay," a song that I had always liked. I didn't even place. So much for solos.

Our first tenor, Wayne Arthur, was an excellent singer, and consistently won the blue ribbons in vocal competition. He was one of the very few that I have known whose voice harmonized beautifully and still was of solo quality.

The rest of us—Harold Arthur, baritone, Velda (who wanted to be called Ed) Masterson, and I—were perfectly willing to let Wayne have all the glory associated with solos. Velda was an excellent bassist. I usually sang the lead and did virtually all of the arrangements.

One of our biggest moments came when we were invited to participate in a "home talent show" sponsored by radio station WLS. The show was held in Pontiac and consisted of individuals and groups who were to, in effect, imitate some or all of the very well-known WLS Barn Dance personalities. A representative had visited the surrounding communities, giving interested performers an opportunity to audition for the big show. The Harmony Four auditioned and were accepted.

It is about sixty miles from Lincoln to Pontiac, but we had the loan of Velda Masterson's father's car, a Model A Ford coupe with a rumble seat. I wish everyone could have the opportunity to ride sixty miles (120, round trip) in a Model A Ford's rumble seat.

It is too bad that rumble seats died a natural death in the later car models.

At the show, the stage was crowded with performers. It looked as if every Tom, Dick, and Harry was trying for a career in the performing arts. The auditorium was packed, wall to wall, with parents, family, friends, and sweethearts of the entertainers, making it look as if all the people in north-central Illinois were there.

There was no one there that we knew, but we agreed that there was one group that we would like to know. Eventually, it was our turn to perform. That was a lucky thing, because we dreaded the long wait that we would have to be on near the end. We did OK, and got a good round of applause. The audience wasn't tired yet, either.

Soon, the group that we were interested in took its turn. It was the Asper Sisters, and they were fine. Suffice it to say, after the show, we all got acquainted, and their parents invited us to their home for refreshments. We accepted and had a very nice time until we finally had to head for home.

We got to Lincoln just in time for Velda's father to leave for the post office to start his mail route. I got home just as Dad was coming out of the house to do the morning chores. The sun was just coming up.

I corresponded with one of the girls for several months but Pontiac was too far away for any meaningful relationship.

We were not invited to become a part of the famous WLS family, and as far as I know, neither was anyone else that appeared on the talent scout program at Pontiac that night. As for me, it was certainly not time wasted. The experience was a part of my education, and I learned one thing about show business: join the union and get yourself a good manager!

Senior Year

My senior year was a little bit dull. As I remember it, a lot of the glamor of new adventures was gone. The new problems I faced were of a more practical nature and I didn't know how to handle them. I also knew that my first responsibility was finishing high school. From there on, I would have to make decisions about my future, but I decided to just take them one at a time.

I knew that the work that I did on the farm was something I did for my folks in exchange for room and board. That didn't provide spending money, but I had never had any before, so I was not liable to miss it now. Guess again. I decided it would surely be handy.

To partially relieve the situation, I applied for work at the J. C. Penney Company store for the pre-Christmas shopping season.

I was hired. The pay was twenty-one cents per hour. We worked at selling for ten hours. After the store closed, we spent another hour, or sometimes two hours, straightening stock and sweeping the floor. They didn't have a janitor, or, if they did, I didn't see him. We received no pay for the cleaning.

After Christmas Eve, we were paid off and my responsibility to J. C. Penneys was ended.

I don't mean to imply that the store was any worse than any other to work for. Wages were low and profits doubtful in almost any business. The assistant manager at this store was paid fifteen dollars a week, and he worked many more hours than we did. That tells you something about what the Depression was like. Christmas gifts were small, but hearts were big.

When we moved to Illinois in 1921, Grandfather Jackson owned a Buick touring car. I don't know what model it was, (it surely was not new!) but as a child, it was of great interest to me. The windshield was vertical and, of course, the top was attached to it. In addition, leather straps, one on each side, were attached to the top at the windshield and extended foreward and down to the front fender. The horn consisted of a bell-shaped metal section somewhat like a megaphone, attached to a rubber ball. If you squeezed the ball, the horn tooted. Usually. It was a real treat, though, to see Grandpa drive into our barn lot.

It was not long after Grandpa moved to Lincoln that he traded his old car for a newer model, also a Buick and a beautifully designed touring car that made everybody's mouth water, it was so nice. However, as eventually happens to all of us, Grandpa got too old to drive and the car was put in the garage, jacked up, and put on blocks to save the tires. It was just left there for two or three years.

It never occurred to anyone that there was more to putting a car in storage than just saving the tires. Consequently, when my father bought the car, it had suffered considerable damage from neglect. It took a while to recondition it, and it never did run as well as it would have if it had been properly stored, but it was, nevertheless, a sweet running vehicle, and I loved to drive it in spite of brakes only working for the back wheels. This was true of all of the cars of that vintage. Mud and gravel roads took a terrible toll on the old-fashioned brakes and were a major factor influencing the number of accidents caused by cars that just wouldn't stop.

Like most boys (and girls) of high school senior age, I enjoyed going out once in a while with my friends. We were a small community, but most of my associates were somewhat scattered and having a car available was a boon to my social life. It was about this time that Dad decided to sell whole milk instead of just the cream from our herd of nine Holstein cows.

This meant that every morning, two or three ten-gallon milk cans had to be hauled to town to the dairy.

Lee had purchased a 1928 model Whippet especially for this job. When he brought the car home, he came to me and said, "Hab, I just bought you a car." I looked at it, but I was not impressed. That had to be one of the ugliest cars that I had ever seen, and to this day, I still think so.

Well, actually, Lee did most of the deliveries, but I claimed the car, and in months to come, I found the little car well-fitted, not only for hauling milk to the dairy, but for hauling my friends, too. I didn't think I ever had any of my acquaintances even hint that it wasn't satisfactory in every way.

My brother-in-law, Maurice Lalicker, also sold milk to the same dairy, Hegele Brothers, in Lincoln. They made delicious ice cream and had a little ice cream parlor adjoining the dairy office. It was a regular ritual when we chanced to meet there, for Lee, Maurice, and me to line up at the bar for a giant malted milk. At that time, a large milkshake (always chocolate for us) cost ten cents.

When I brought the milk to the dairy before school, I would leave it and go to school, then pick up the cleaned and sterilized cans on the way home.

By this time, I was looking forward to the time when I wouldn't have to get up in the morning (which is itself bad enough) and go milk the cows. I had been milking them since I was ten or eleven years old and I just couldn't see any future in it for me, either with or without the Whippet.

I have to admit, however, that we lived better with the cows than we would have lived without them.

Model T

Lee had worked hard on the farm ever since he got out of school, doing jobs that would tax a man much larger and stronger than he was. The country was fairly well off and prices for grain and livestock had not decreased as much as they would within a few months. It was at this time that Lee came home from town one day, driving a brand new Model T Ford. We were all glad for him, but it was a while before I became aware of the significance of the events that were about to happen.

Lee was dating Miss Bessie Martinie at this time, so the little car was put to good use very quickly.

After Miss Martinie left her job at West Point, she accepted a position at Elkhart, a little town south of Lincoln, on Route 66. This unpaved road came through Lincoln on Fifth Street, out of town west, down a hill past the cemetery, across Salt Creek and on toward Springfield. In the spring, it could be mighty muddy and slick, even if it was Route 66, and it was a lot easier to get down the hill than it was to get back up, as Lee found out after taking Bessie to Elkhart after a date one Sunday evening.

The Model T did not have gears like other cars, but instead had three pedals on the floor which controlled friction: one acted as brakes, one for reverse, and one for forward. They usually worked like a charm . . . until they wore out.

When Lee came to "Cemetery Hill" on the way home, he pressed the pedal to engage the "low" speed. The low portion of the band was worn out and he had to turn around and back up the hill to more level ground.

This was not an unusual occurrence for Model T owners, even though there were few hills in Logan County, there was, at certain times of the year, plenty of mud, which taxed the newest "bands."

The Model T had two levers on the steering wheel column, just below the steering wheel. The lever on the right side of the column was to regulate the speed. To accelerate, you just pulled the lever down until the engine reached the desired speed. The lever on the left regulated the "spark," or the timing, up for retarding the timing to start the engine or run at very low speeds; down for accelerated speeds.

On older models that had to be cranked by hand to start them, the spark lever had to be up. If it was not, the engine was likely to backfire, the engine would be quickly reversed, and somebody was likely to have a broken arm. It was interesting to see those who had been careless walking around the town square on Saturday night with their right arm in a cast!

The Model T deserves a special place in our history and in the development of the automotive industry. Many a young man discovered the fine points of the internal combustion engine and other feature repairs and operations resulting from operating and repairing this famous little car, which helped in many ways to bridge the gap between horse and buggy days and the later, more modern, machine age.

Even as a child, I could see the problem that Dad and Lee had remembering to grease, change oil regularly, maintain tires, and all of the other things that machines required that were not required of horse-drawn equipment. Adjusting to gradual change is difficult enough, but the machine age seemed to come to us so quickly!

The late 1920s and early 30s was an interesting time to be "growing up." It was for me, although I didn't fully appreciate it at the time.

Fortunately, we had a radio. Listening to the news was a regular event. We usually came in from the field work at 11:30, which gave us time to water and feed the horses or service the tractor before going into the house for the noon meal.

We listened to the market report and the weather forecast which were topics of value to farmers. Conversation was limited because we were hungry, but that didn't interfere with our listening.

We got along fine without the pictures. One part of this routine I remember vividly. It was the market report given by a very fine man, Mr. Jim Poole. It went like this:

> This is WLS, the Sears-Roebuck station, broadcasting the Chicago Board of Trade Grain and Provision Market Quotations direct from the WLS studios in the Chicago Board of Trade Building. The markets at present;—;—;—;—Done all in one breath!

It was a privilege for me a few years later to be present in the studio for that Dinner Bell program market report.

Later, WLS was operated by a farm organization (I think, the Farm Bureau) and was my favorite radio station for many years. We regularly listened to the Barn Dance on Saturday night and to the Dinner Bell program all through my adolescent years. Later, I was a guest on both programs.

This was a time when our lives were changing, almost imperceptably at first, but gradually awakening awareness of things to come. From going to town on Saturday night or discussing the drought in the west, we began to broaden our horizons through awareness of things happening all over the country, or even the world.

We all knew about airplanes. Occasionally, a barnstormer would make a trip to our county and take people for a short ride in his antique biplane. The going rate for some was "penny a pound" depending, of course, on the length of the flight. I sure did want to go, but I didn't even get as far as asking Dad for the price. I only weighed about ninety pounds.

I had read about the air-mail and how it was growing, and had read a book about a boy who took up flying and became an air-mail pilot. Our place was located just right for planes flying between Chicago and St. Louis to come right over our farm, usually just a little way south of our house. When we heard one coming, I would always run out into the yard to see it, wondering if it was an air-mail plane or something else.

It was about this time that the name Lindberg appeared frequently in the paper and was heard in the radio news. Word of his proposed flight intrigued me and I knew that he had to be the pilot of some of the planes that flew over our place.

Some of them were flying pretty low, and I always waved at the pilot. If any of them saw me, they didn't wave back.

We all followed every move he made as they were reported in the paper or on the radio during the flight and for many months after that, including his marriage to Ann Morrow, the kidnapping and murder of their first infant son, and the trial and execution of Bruno Richard Hauptmann, the murderer.

Although two pilots (Alcock and Brown) had flown non-stop eight years before, Lindy was the first to fly it alone. This trip and his other great contributions to flying were big enough to make him my number-one boyhood hero, but just as great was the kind of person that he was.

Of course, the news in the early 1920s was not all great and beautiful. There was Al Capone. Al was a dishwasher in a cabaret. Apparently, he didn't like that job, and took up "gangstering." He did alright as a gangster. We know that because he lived so long with people shooting at him. He started out in 1920 and washed out in the late thirties. Believe me, he was not one of my boyhood heroes. Actually, I have a little trouble keeping boyhood heroes. Rear Admiral Byrd didn't take me to the South Pole in 1929, I found Gene Tunney and Jack Dempsey to be disappointments (they became Navy Officers in World War II).

The one who never disappointed me was Will Rogers.

Amelia Earhart was really high on my totem pole. Our newspaper informed us of her route and time that she would be over Logan County on her coast to coast flight to break the speed record. She flew over our place and was out of sight so quickly it scared us. Over two hundred miles per hour! We were all sorry to hear of her disappearance and death.

Our radio was battery-powered and it had to be charged often when events like these were happening.

1929 came in as a good year. Prices for farm produce were good, and while no one in our neighborhood was getting rich, no one was starving, either. News items from the east were encouraging and indicated confidence that the economy would continue to be satisfactory, or even grow.

However, early in September, there began a slowdown that made some investors uneasy about the immediate future. By the end of October, the crash came and the Great Depression was underway, resulting in a period of suffering as great as anyone in modern times had ever known.

It is not for me to discuss the history of those times other than its effect on me and our friends and neighbors. Volumes have been written about it, but only those who lived through it can really understand what it was really like. Here are a few examples:

> Ten cents a bushel for corn (corn that had cost the farmer from thirty to fifty cents to produce).

Wheat under one dollar per bushel: Income per acre, none.
One pair of J. C. Penney overalls to wear to school: $2.50.
One small hamburger: ten cents.
Giant malted milk: twenty cents.
A cup of coffee: five cents.
A bowl of chili: ten cents.
Annual farm income: under four hundred dollars for the year.

Many farmers didn't break even. Thousands and thousands of people were begging for food, regardless of their education or competence.

We had no money to spend for luxuries. If I was lucky, Dad would give me a quarter to spend when we went to town. I hated to go to town, but after working in the fields all week, that quarter looked pretty good and I made no objection. I usually headed for the Western Hotel, which was a combination pool hall, soft-drink parlor, hotel for itinerant field hands, and weekly meetings for many of the farmers in West Lincoln township. It served as a good place for workers to meet prospective employers, or to make inquiries as to who might need hired help. Hired hands met there on Saturday night to go "out on the town" with fellows their own age. They worked a six-day week and were ready for a break.

I would take my quarter and buy a coke (a nickel), a Hershey bar (another nickel), and a *Western Story Magazine* (fifteen cents), go to the back room, which was the pool room, and sit in one of the chairs which were lined up along the side of the room. I would eat my candy, drink my Coca Cola, read, and wait for the folks to finish their shopping and come for me. It was a real high old time.

I remember saying to Lee one time, "There is going to be a day when I am going to have either a candy bar, a bottle of 'pop' or a dish of ice cream every day!"

Lee laughed, but didn't say a word. I think he thought that there would never be a day when we could afford such a thing.

We made it. There are not many days when I don't have at least one of the above, and frequently, all of them!

It may seem strange, but we never considered ourselves poor. We had plenty of meat (pork, beef, and chicken), a huge garden with all the things we liked best, and apple and peach trees in the orchard to supply canned fruit for the winter. We had a separate potato patch, and we would have the bins in the basement filled with them while the shelves in the pantry held dozens of cans of tomatoes, beets, green beans, greens and assorted small fruits, jams and jellies.

One winter, we had a storm. Sleet coated the trees with ice, breaking the branches and ruining most of the fruit trees that we needed so badly and that my grandfather was so proud of. Lee and I got a good workout sawing the ruined trees with a two-man crosscut saw.

That summer, Dad had to buy peaches which came from southern Illinois and pay three dollars a bushel for them. I thought that was too much, but I got straightened out real quickly about the needs for the coming winter.

There was no ice delivery to the farms and electrically powered refrigerators were just beginning to be widely used. Electric power lines had not reached us, and even if they had, we could not have paid an electric bill, or have had the buildings wired.

We had never had it; so we didn't miss it.

Home Life

Depression or not, we were able to maintain stable relationships within the family, as well as with the neighbors and nearby relatives. We always accepted our lot as our way of life, and that would never change, except possibly to make our bonds stronger.

Mom continued to prepare her delicious Sunday dinners. She had Clarice to help her. She had lived at our house with her two boys, Norman and Kenneth, since she and her husband, Herbert Cecil, parted. I grew up with the boys and that made them seem more like brothers than nephews, and this feeling grew stronger over the years.

Frances and her husband, Maurice, and eventually their little daughter, Marcellen (Marcie) were always there. Heaven only knew who else might show up. Frequently, it was my mother's niece, Pearl Yocum, and her family or Jack and Floy Wroughton (our pastor) and their little daughter, Diverle, and possibly some farmhands who dropped in for a visit.

We had a large dining table and managed to load it with food for the small crowd around it.

In the summer months, we frequently had a freezer of homemade ice cream. We had all kinds of the "makings" at home except for the ice. We would gather up some old quilts or sacks, go into Lincoln to the ice plant, get a fifty-pound block, wrap it so it wouldn't melt, and head for home and the ice-cream freezer.

On Winter nights when the evenings were longer, there was usually a card game such as seven-up, pitch, or pinochle.

Mom, however, had memories of the attitude of some preachers about the great sin of card playing. So, when she thought that the preacher was coming, she would "hide" the deck of cards.

My fun-loving sisters thought this was pretty funny, and couldn't help telling Jack Wroughton about it. He was a fun-lover, too, and kept a straight face, remaining silent about it until Christmas, when he bought Mom a new deck of cards.

All of my family were readers. Our biggest problem was finding books, so we did a lot of exchanging with the neighbors. One time, Dad had a copy of Zane Grey's *Man of the Forest*. We were all in the parlor, enjoying the warmth and light from our large base burner, a huge, fed-from-the-top, isinglass windowed stove that seemed to radiate comfort to be in its very presence.

Dad finished the book, laid it aside, and said, "That is really a great story. I think it will make Grey famous."

"What was it about?" we wanted to know.

"Well, I'll tell you," was the answer. And he did, *almost word for word, the entire book.* I think that this was one of the most enjoyable evenings that I ever spent, and I think about it every time I read the book, which has been many times. He was wrong, however, about Zane Grey being made famous by that book. He was already one of the most famous "Western" writers and still is. He is one of several who helped fill the market demand for the western romance, which remains popular even today. After all of these years, I still read old books: *Ramona, The Shepherd of the Hills, The Mine with the Iron Door* and others that I grew up with.

I cannot see that reading Westerns hurt my character very much. Perhaps I neglected some chores so I could read?

Good times were not always restricted to the home base. There was a tradition of long-standing that was observed by several, if not all, of my mother's near relatives. Her nieces, Pearl Yokum and Fanny Short and their families, nephew John (Dad) Rankin and family and all of our family would have a regular outdoor reunion on the Labor Day weekend. The favored spot was a place named Rocky Ford on Salt Creek, near Lincoln. The Rankin brothers and their sister, in-laws of my mother's sister, Laura, lived on a farm bordering the creek and allowed us all to camp, fish, and spend the weekend there.

In the early 1920s Salt Creek was a clean stream which flowed from its source in McClean County southwesterly through DeWitt County to Logan (at Lincoln) and on to its mouth, joining the Sangamon River. It was a beautiful stream with fairly clear water and a good population of catfish and carp.

The men would fish most of the day and all night, and there would be a fish-fry on Sunday. Most of the fish were carp caught on throw-lines and checked regularly through the night. It was a wonderful, fun weekend for everybody. The ladies slept in the big Rankin barn and the men did the best they could. It seemed that there was only one thing that you could depend on without fail: it was bound to rain!

Over the years, Salt Creek became so polluted with sewage from upstream that it was no longer fit for this type of recreation. The Ford became a limestone quarry, and the reunion was moved to a place called Fisher's Ford on Sugar Creek.

As the older folks passed on, the reunion lost its attraction and became part of our past.

On the farm of the 1930s, the work days were long and many of the jobs had to be done without the aid of efficient tools and equipment. This was just as true of the housework as it was for the necessary outdoor chores.

We are all probably familiar with the old-fashioned washboard. It probably was the first "washing machine" to be used, and certainly the most common, except for beating the clothes with a stick as I have seen it done along the banks of a stream in Mexico. I won't comment on the method of operation here, as it is well-known. Incidentally, we have used them many times on extended camping trips. They are effective, light, and easy to carry, plus, they are cheap!

Washing machines used in rural areas, and especially homes without electricity, came in assorted sizes and shapes. They all, however, had one thing in common; they had a tub of some kind to hold the hot water (and Grandma's lye soap) and some other part that rubbed the clothes. Bleach as we know it today was unknown then, so white things had "blueing" added to the rinse water. Without the "blueing" white clothes came out of the rinse in a sickly-looking yellow. Some of the overalls and other heavy articles of clothing had to be boiled to get them clean.

Our kitchen became a laundry every Monday. The machine was brought in and buckets of soft water were carried in from the cistern which was out in the yard. The water was poured into a copper oval-shaped "boiler," which was on the cook stove and brought to a near boiling temperature, then it was put into the tub part of the washing machine. The clothes were put in and rubbed until they were judged clean. After everything was washed, the machine was drained into buckets and carried outdoors again. The rinse water was carried in, heated, and poured into the machine, then the clothes were put through the "wringer" to squeeze the water out so they could be carried outdoors to the clothesline for drying.

My mother liked to have a sunny day for drying the clothes, as the sunlight helped to bleach the white things. If the white clothes were not *snow* white, they were not hung out until further work on them made them snow white. Mom always thought she could tell a lot about a new neighbor by the way that the clothes looked on the line. In at least one instance, she waited until after she had a chance to see a wash on the line before she made a social call.

We didn't have a basement under the house that Grandpa Jackson built. There was a one-room "cellar" for storing fruit and potatoes, but that was all it was good for. One year, Dad and Lee dug out enough to make a furnace room and a room for coal. Dad bought a big coal-burning furnace and had it installed, putting an end to heating the house with stoves that had to be "put up" in the fall and "taken down" in the spring. It was always such a relief to get rid of the stoves and enjoy the added room to move around and to rearrange the furniture. We did, however, sadly miss sitting around them in the winter nights, especially the old base-burner and its bed of hot coals that could be seen through the isinglass window.

The advent of the new laundry room revolutionized wash day. Dad bought a two-tub washer with a power-operated agitator and wringer. You could wash the clothes in one tub, wring them out and let them fall into the rinse tub, then wring them again before carrying them upstairs onto the south porch and into the house. The water could now be drained through a floor drain installed by Dad and Lee when the basement was dug. However, the water still had to be heated in the kitchen and carried to the basement.

The power problem was solved by purchasing a one-cylinder gas engine which was mounted on a four-wheeled "truck." The engine belt pulley-operated a drive shaft going into the basement from outside, powering the machine.

On days other than wash day, the engine was pulled to the barn well that furnished water for the livestock. On days when the wind was not strong enough to turn the windmill, we could start up the engine (hopefully) and pump water into the redwood stock tank. Unfortunately, I was the one usually elected to move the engine the three hundred-and-a-few feet between the two pump locations. At that time, I weighed about seventy-five or eighty pounds, so winter *or* summer, I worked up a good sweat . . . especially if it was muddy or if there was snow on the ground.

The summer passed on and soon we were husking corn. If there ever was a job that worked up an appetite, corn "shucking" is one. Lee and I worked together. We had three wagons and teams, and hired men took two of them. Also, I have to admit the neither of the "Jackson boys" were any great shakes as corn huskers.

The weather was nearly always cool in the early fall and the corn stalks and shucks were dry. These were the good days. When it was drizzling rain or if, in the early morning, the stalks were covered with frost, it was not so funny. Later in the season, we were likely to have snow, or even ice. Of course, we wore shucking gloves or mittens, but when they got wet, your hands got cold and stiff and the skin chapped and got sore. Shuckers sometimes sprained their wrists throwing the heavy ears of corn into the wagon. Not only was a sprained wrist painful, it broke your rhythm, which is very important if you are trying to get your load finished and have a respectable number of bushels. Many good shuckers tried to get one hundred bushels per day: sometimes two full loads and a partial load before dark.

By the time that the wagons were unloaded, the horses unharnessed and put in the barn to be fed, and you staggered to the house for supper, you knew that you had done a day of work, and had earned every penny that you hired out for. We paid our shuckers four cents a bushel, which was customary most years during the thirties.

The straight-standing stalks, with the ears a uniform height above ground, have been developed as a result of hybridization and would have been a paradise for the 1930s husker. We had a lot of the stalks broken off and the ears laying on the ground, sometimes covered with frost or snow. The husker had to stoop to pick them up before he stripped them of the husks and could throw them in the wagon.

After the wagon was loaded, the corn was hauled to the corn crib for storage until the grain was dried and ready for the market.

The corn cribs were constructed with a huge "room" on each side of a main driveway. The walls of the driveway had drop-doors on the bottom of each wall so the corn could be raked out into the "feeder" troughs, which contained an endless chain with cross-drags. These dragged the ears to the corn sheller, which separated the grain from the cobs, stacked (piled) the cobs in a neat pile and ran the shelled corn into the wagon or truck to be hauled to the railroad elevator.

In the corn belt, the days of the transient corn shucker are gone, and huge combines are doing the work, not only husking the corn, but shelling it, too. Believe me, it is better now.

On Grandpa's old farm, the corn cribs, built to hold a thousand bushels on each side, are gone. Indeed, the end of my high-school years marked the end of an era, not only for me, but for the lives of all of my family and eventually for all farmers in the midwest.

Life certainly was not all drudgery. Lee, Maurice, and I had always enjoyed going down to the creek and fishing all night. By this time, our nephew, Kenny Cecil, who had always lived with his mother and brother at our house, was old enough to be an active participant, and Lee's son, Davey, also got initiated about this time.

We were very close. We had lived and worked together for so long that we nearly always thought in terms of "we" instead of "I."

We used pole and line part of the time, but "throw lines" were our best bet. We used a heavy cord long enough to reach across the creek, with short drop-lines at regular intervals for the entire length. We baited the hooks on the droplines with worms, bacon rinds, or anything we could find without buying it. Soft newly formed grains of corn was effective for carp. . . . At least it was supposed to be. We never caught enough to find out, but we thoroughly enjoyed every minute of those trips.

If I could relive any day of my past life, I would choose to spend the night part of it on the banks of Sugar Creek at Fisher's Ford with my very dear "pards."

Time for College

Graduation from high school and the associated activities did not affect me in the way that I expected. I remember as the time approached, my first feelings were not regret at having to leave that environment because of any personal attachments, but instead a desire to remain to take so many of the classes that I didn't have time for in the four short years.

After graduation, I spent the rest of the summer on the farm. We had improved our methods and some of the drudgery had been replaced with better equipment. We had replaced the Old Fordson tractor with a McCormick-Deering 15-30 when the old Case threshing machine was traded in on a new one. It was smaller and could be powered with the farm tractors that Carl Baker, Ed Schroeder, and Dad used for their regular work.

Many of the farmers had cultivated the young corn plants with cultivators built for cleaning two rows at a time. We still used the old one-row, well-worn machines that Dad had purchased from Grandpa Jackson in 1921.

It was about this time that Dad bought a little F-12 Farmall tractor that would cultivate two rows at a time. It didn't need to rest or be cooled off when it was hot, but as long as it had gasoline, water and a little grease, it could work from "can see" to "can't see." Lee and I took turns during the day keeping the little tractor humming, stopping only to refuel. We could cultivate forty acres in a day with a lot less effort than it took to do much less than that with the horse-drawn equipment.

After the corn harvest was completed, life settled into the Winter routine. It consisted mainly of milking the cows, delivering the milk, making the ever-needed repairs and, for me, being bored.

Gone was the great desire for knowledge that made me dread leaving high school and gone was the satisfaction that I had always found sufficient in my association with my family. Lee now had family of his own, my nephew Kenney Cecil was in high school and had his own friends and his trombone (which he played beautifully). I didn't see my friends often, although I did see Boyd Read occasionally. One weekend, he came out to the farm. It was winter, so instead of getting out and doing something, we were content to just visit. My folks always treated my friends as if they were members of the family, so we thoroughly enjoyed ourselves.

On Sunday afternoon, we were all sitting in the parlor, and things were pretty quiet. Suddenly, Boyd said, "Why don't you go to school with me tomorrow? It will give you a chance to see some of the folks that we knew in high school."

It was nearing the end of the first semester, and I thought the teachers might not appreciate any intrusion, but Boyd said it would not be a problem, so I agreed to go.

I don't remember which classes I visited with Boyd, but it doesn't really matter because everything was running smoothly. It was far enough into the semester to be comfortable in the classroom environment, but not near enough to final exam time to feel end-of-term stress. I enjoyed the day immensely.

We spent some time between classes meeting some of the students from other localities, and I was impressed with their general attitude about the school. I could see at a glance that it was quite different from high school, although I had known that it would be, the students here had the responsibility for their own attitude and mastery of the subject matter.

Suddenly, I realized that I had been missing the association with my own age group and a chance to be part of an academic environment.

I had a tendency to make decisions quickly, weighing various factors, sorting out the doubts and, if possible, acting without beating around the bush. I have been "caught up short" a few times, but over the years, it seems for me to be the best.

The president of Lincoln College at that time was a fine man named Benjamin Moore. His student secretary was a girl I had met that morning, and she introduced me to Mr. Moore, setting the stage adroitly for finding out what I wanted to know . . . for instance, if there was any way that I could attend school the next semester. The student secretary, standing off to one side of Mr. Moore, was trying not to laugh. She knew some things that I didn't, like how desperate the college was for students.

I can't remember who the secretary was. I had met too many students that day to remember them, but it well could have been Alice Cave. Whoever it was did me a good turn that day, giving me moral support in a mighty strange environment. Little did I know at that time that fifty years later I, along with Elvira Hoepfner, a young lady also in that class, would be awarded "honor graduate" status and that the offices of college and university presidents would no longer be strange to me.

Room and board was no problem. I could live at home. The tuition was seventy dollars a semester, but I could pay half of it in cash and work for the college at thirty cents an hour for the remaining thirty-five dollars. I must buy my books, but sometimes, they could be purchased from students who had finished the course. Cars could not be driven on the campus grounds and must be parked on the campus parking lot. I was also to make arrangements with Mr. Irving E. W. Olson for the work that I was to do on the campus. I decided to find Mr. Olson later. I had enough for one day, and that afternoon Boyd went home to Broadwell and I went home to break the news to my family. No one seemed surprised or curious. I guess they just expected me to break out about this time.

The next day, I went to the First National Bank in Lincoln, borrowed thirty-five dollars, and got Dad to sign the note. Next, I made arrangements to sell what as left of my 4-H club livestock. There were four slightly over two hundred pound barrows ready for market. I got four cents a pound for them. That bought all of my books but one. I was taking General Botany, and of course, that was one of the more expensive texts that I would need. *Well,* I thought, *maybe something would turn up.*

Yes, indeed, something *did* turn up!

Finally, the new semester started, and I was right in the middle of it. While I was waiting for my first meeting of Economics 101, several students were lounging on the steps that led to the second level. This class was only offered once a year, so the enrollment was usually large. I am not sure, but I believe that it was a required subject.

Everyone was relaxed and enjoying themselves when we all looked toward the top of the stairs to see a young woman starting toward us. I don't remember anyone saying anything except the usual greetings, and I had given only a brief glance at her, when I thought I heard a voice say, *That is the girl you are going to marry.*

Now, I had not given girls too much of a thought since graduating from high school, and I certainly never in my life up to that time had thought about marriage! I took a quick look around to see which smart alec was being funny, but there was no one that wasn't occupied with something else. I also knew, or at least thought I did, that the thought did not originate with me! Besides, the thought, or voice, did not say, "*I* am going to marry." It said, *"You* are going to marry." Another disturbing fact was that the voice (if that is what it was) was neither masculine nor feminine. Anyway, by the time I recovered, the bell had rang and we were all headed for Economics. This event took place in February, 1935. As of the date of this writing, sixty-six years ago, and until this time, I have never told this story to anyone. Not even that young lady, who said that her name was Joy Boatman.

We made our way into the classroom, where we were met by a chubby little individual who took the roll. I took a seat in the front row. The new girl took the seat next to me, filling the front row.

Apparently, the students that had been in school the preceding term had some idea about what the class would be like . . . either the subject matter or the teacher, because the more experienced ones took the seats in the rear of the room near the door that opened to the large hall. I didn't notice at the time that the seats in the two back rows were all occupied by women. The full impact of this situation didn't hit me until several days later.

I had the textbook for this course, and actually enjoyed reading it. I was completely ignorant of the multiple facets involved in handling money or conducting any kind of business transaction. Perhaps, if I studied really hard, I could find out how to get rich.

It didn't help.

The teacher opened his copy of the text, leaned both elbows on the podium, and began to lecture. At least, I think he was trying to convince the students that he was lecturing, but he didn't fool anyone. He was reading most of the hour directly from the text.

Apparently, the students had known what to expect and had not bothered to read the assignment.

Joy, sitting next to me, finally suggested that we share her botany book and my economics text. It was a good deal for both of us.

We also were laboratory partners and worked as one of the teams that tackled a semester project. Our project was to collect the leaves, twigs, and other morphological characteristics and match them to the proper section of a diagnostic taxonomic key. I used the key many years later in high-school biology classes.

I am glad that I got that Economics class out of the way when I did. It was a real disappointment and I hoped my other classes would be more like what I thought a college class would be. The botany class seemed to meet my requirement to a "T". Joy and I both enjoyed the subject matter and the teacher, Mr. Emil P. Kruschke, was excellent. He had studied at the University of Wisconsin and had completed the course work requirements for his doctorate. He planned to later work for one of the museums if a position opened up. I believe that he did work in that or some related area after he left Lincoln College. I lost track of him for a while, but finally heard from his brother-in-law that he had died. Joy and I were greatly saddened by the news . . . for ourselves, and for his wife, Ruth Bliss, a Lincoln girl and former Lincoln College student.

Other courses were taught by competent instructors, and English, Mathematics, Zoology, Hygiene, Chemistry, Physics, Music and Art were, for the most part, exactly what I wanted to study. The teachers would help you any way they could if you really needed it, but they encouraged the students to be as independent as possible. As Lee used to say: "Saddle your own broncs!"

I had continued my interest in music, but Harold and Wayne Arthur were still in high school and we didn't have time for much singing. I joined the mixed chorus as there was not enough interest from the small student body for a men's glee club. I enjoyed the chorus, but missed the camaraderie of the men's group and the type of songs they would sing.

I signed up for the course in "harmony" as I knew so little about it and it was fundamental for arranging. The teacher was a young man who was well-versed in music theory, but illiterate in how to teach and how to relate to students, especially the men. I stuck it out for four or five weeks, but by that time, I was hopelessly lost. I went to the Dean and asked for permission to drop the class. He asked some questions, and by his manner, I could tell that he knew enough about the situation to give me the permission slip to give to the instructor. I did that, and never went to that class again.

However, when the grades came out, there was my harmony course with a D grade. So many had dropped the course that the teacher did not want to worsen his reputation any more than it was, so he kept me on the roll. I hated to have a D on my records, but as far as I can tell, it has never hurt my scholastic reputation. The teacher left Lincoln College that Spring.

The college may have been small and had its problems with a couple of faculty members, but that was a normal situation in depression-wracked private schools everywhere.

I worked out my thirty-five dollar tuition debt pushing a sixteen-inch reel-type lawn mower to and fro over about two or three square blocks of lawn. Power lawn mowers of that time were "man-power" mowers, but I ended the Spring semester with my debt clear and that much more to apply on the coming fall term. I was grateful for the opportunity, and owe a lot to Mr. George Daniels, caretaker of grounds and landscapes, and his little Spitz dog, Toby, for helping me in so many ways (like sharpening the mower blades) and at times creating jobs to help me earn a little extra. He was known to faculty and students alike as George and the use of his first name without the Mister didn't seem over-familiar or disrespectful. He liked the students, and only in rare instances did he let it be known that he disapproved of anyone.

George lived alone in a little house on the campus. I knew nothing of his past life, and cared even less, but I sensed that at times he was lonely and needed the association with the students. He liked to go to the theater and attended nearly all of the movies, at least all that had his favorite stars, and frequently would treat one or more students to the show . . . especially if they had a car, for the campus was a long walk from the theater and George had done a full day's work.

My partnership with Joy had continued, and I finally got up enough courage to ask her for a date. We went to a movie, had a snack after, and both of us enjoyed the evening. So much in one evening was a rare thing for us, and in later years, we commented about it frequently.

In the Spring, usually about Eastertime, the college had a nice dress-up dance. I think it was called the Spring Fling. That event led to our second date, and a few days later, an invitation to spend

Easter with her family on the farm near Shumway, which was about a hundred miles south of Lincoln. In addition to her father and mother, there were two sisters, Verna Louise (she didn't like that name and changed it for all practical purposes to Sue), Elizabeth, the youngest of the children, and Carl, who was a couple years older than Elizabeth.

You can be sure I got a good "once-over" from the youngsters and Verna, who waited until she was away from home to become Sue. Dan and Bethyl kept their feelings to themselves. That was probably a good thing.

On Easter Sunday, several families of relatives came for Easter dinner and I guess we all passed muster, at least I didn't hear anything contrary.

It did not take long for me to feel at home on the campus and in the classrooms. Everything went according to my expectations and I was doing well, except in the music class already mentioned. I would not, however, want anyone to get the idea that the students were angels. I am quite sure that if you looked closely, you would find that angels were very scarce! This was especially noticeable, as you might expect, in the early Spring, when young men's fancy lightly turns to thoughts of almost anything but academics, and the same thing is true of young women.

We had all conscientiously attended our Economics class even though it had not improved to any appreciable extent. The instructor just as conscientiously took the roll as soon as everyone was seated, then, as usual, buried his face in the textbook and told us what the author wrote. Of course, we had quit reading the text long before, only referring to it to brush up on something that we thought we ought to know. Sometimes, I studied it and found it pretty interesting.

Mr. Irving Olson and his wife had for several years treated all of the students in their classes to a cook-out breakfast to celebrate May Day. Joy was in Olson's class in Physiology and since the Olsons knew "how the land lay" between Joy and me, she was told she might invite me to attend the picnic. This was an early-in-the-morning affair, because several of us had our Economics class at eight o'clock. We made the appointment all right, but were needing a little primping after our breakfast.

Everyone came into the classroom as usual, the roll was taken, and the lecture proceeded in the usual routine, but with one modification: the women in the back row (I think all of them had been at the Olson breakfast) gently folded their books, bent down as low as they could, and quietly stole out of the classroom through the rear door and into the main hall. Those of us in the front of the room were unaware of the exodus until, just before the end of the hour they all came marching back into the classroom through that same rear door. They were washed, combed, polished, and all traces of an outdoor breakfast were removed. They all looked as innocent as doves.

The instructor picked up his class record book, saw that he had recorded them as present, then left the room. I felt sorry for him, but as far as I know, nothing was ever said about the fiasco, to him or anyone else. I would like to say that the teacher got help and changed his ways, but I can't say that because he never did.

We all passed the course. So much for angels. God bless them, every one!

Gradually the semester ended, final exams were passed, and it was time for me to get back to helping on the farm. Farm routines seldom varied from year to year and you knew that on a given week of any month you would be doing a specific job. Depending, of course, on the weather. Farmers frequently preface a statement of intentions with, "If it isn't raining (snowing, sleeting, etc.)," or just saying, "If it's fit." Fit meaning the weather in general or the effect of past weather, such as ankle-deep mud after a summer storm.

In the middle-western corn belt, the weather can go from the sublime to the ridiculous at the drop of your hat, and if you don't grab fast, your hat will be blown off before you can drop it. April and May can be cold and damp for a few days; followed by very hot. June can be very hot, followed by very cool. I used to think that the lines: *"What is so rare as a day in June, then if ever, come perfect days"* should be: *"What is so rare as a day in June, at least one that is fit to be outdoors."*

We were always cultivating corn in June, and riding a horse-drawn cultivator can be a cold job when a cold front moves in from the north even if it is June. One time we were working in a field that had been planted to corn the preceding year. Some of the old shucks and stalks had been blown to the end of the rows and lodged in the Osage Orange hedge fence. We were so cold that we gathered up a pile of the plant residue and built a small fire. I will always remember how good it felt and how glad we were when quitting time came and we could go to the barn and get warm.

The rest of the summer was uneventful. I did, however, appreciate the opportunity to help Dad and Lee with the farm work. All of the years that I had been in school, Lee had to do not only his own work, but in addition, the work that I would have done if I had been available. While I was concerned about the extra work thrown on my brother, I knew that he wanted me to go ahead and prepare myself as well we could afford. It didn't take an Einstein to see that one little hundred and forty acre farm could not support three families. It had reached its limit with two, and mine would have been the third. So, I, the youngest son, stayed in school. I do not mean to imply that I would have been forced out. If I had wanted to stay and farm with Dad and Lee, I could have and I knew that all the time. The decision was mine. I think that I made the right one, and I think that this summer was truly the one where I "crossed over."

Even though I never set foot on the college campus that summer, there were some of the wheels grinding along with events that affected me, although I did not recognize them at that time.

Joy and I had a very close relationship with Mr. and Mrs. Irving E. W. Olson. Joy had taken one class and was impressed with his knowledge of subject matter and his ability to teach it. I had worked with him in our student programs taken to area high schools to promote Lincoln College. The college needed all of the promotion it could get, and we tried our best to make the area students and faculty of the schools we visited cognizant of the true value of Lincoln College.

Irving was finishing his master's degree work at Northwestern University. He planned to do more extensive research which would take two summers of field studies before he could finish his dissertation. The field work was done in Benzie County, Michigan, and included an in-depth study of some of the area. This made it imperative that he spend that summer (1935) and the next summer in Michigan completing the research and writing the dissertation.

Olson's faculty advisor was Dr. W. G. Waterman from Northwestern University in Evanston. The Watermans owned a summer home and two small cottages near the little village of Crystallia on Crystal Lake and near the Lake Michigan shore. The Olsons lived in one of the cottages, located conveniently for access to the bogs and to Irving's faculty advisor.

The Watermans planned for some college-student help for the summer, and through the Olsons, offered Joy an opportunity to go north and help Mrs. Waterman. Joy needed a summer job, and this worked out nicely for everyone.

I heard from Joy occasionally through the summer, and knew that she liked the Watermans very much and that she was enjoying her working vacation. I don't know how much money she was paid, but she had her room and board, so whatever she was paid, it was all available for her to do as she pleased with it.

One afternoon in the latter part of August, we were surprised to see the Olson's car pull into the parking area by our front gate. It took only a glance to see that there was something wrong, and Joy especially had about the most woebegone look that I had ever seen.

When they left Benzie County, they planned to stop briefly at the university to clean up a few odds and ends of business pertaining to Irving's work, then come on home. While waiting for him, Joy and Mrs. Olson (Lona) went shopping. Joy had bought a real nice suit, primarily to wear at some of the college functions, and that was by far the nicest one that she had ever owned.

I don't remember the fine details that followed, but later, sometime when the car was left parked, it was broken into and most, if not all, of their luggage was stolen. It was a heart-breaking experience for both Joy and the Olsons. Teachers at that time were not wealthy, especially those teaching in small church-affiliated schools like Lincoln College, and there was no recovery of the loss.

True to form, Mom fixed a good meal for everyone. The Olsons went to their residence in Lincoln, and Joy stayed at our house overnight, then I took her home so she could have a little time with family before the beginning of the fall semester.

Sophomore Year

I didn't do any lawn mowing in the fall, keeping busy with promotion programs of one kind or another. One addition that delighted me was the presence of Wayne and Harold Arthur, the baritone and first tenor of the *Harmony Four*. The only thing missing was a good bass singer and we knew where there was one if we could get him to fill in. Morris Branom was enrolled at the college and he had been a member of the original double quartet under the direction of Mr. George Brown at Lincoln High School, so we knew that his voice would be compatible with ours. Fortunately, Morris was willing and he fit right in.

It had been some time since we had sang a note together, but after a few hours of practice, we smoothed out and were ready to show off if we could find anyone who was willing to listen to us.

I had been working with Irving Olson to get student talent for promotion trips to some of the high schools, so it was easy for me to arrange an occasional off-campus performance. That was a good thing for us, because, no matter how much practice you get in private sessions, there was nothing better than a live audience to make you really smooth out the rough spots.

There was a new music teacher this year, a pretty young woman named Dorothy Sharp. She was primarily a voice teacher and she was very helpful, especially in helping us make arrangements for new musical numbers. Arranging was always difficult for us and we appreciated the help. As previously noted, the course I had started the year before did not appreciatively add to my knowledge of music theory and I didn't know much to start with.

I was beginning to suspect that music might not be the best choice of a career, and it might be a good idea if I explored the field more thoroughly. I think that my interest in science, and especially anything related to the natural outdoor world, was beginning to exert its influence. Once again, I remembered the advice of my much-loved brother-in-law when he urged me to "take chemistry!"

and for the second time, I did. This time, it was at the college level and under the direction of the Dean of the college, Mr. Carl Schilz.

That is the point in my life at which I really felt secure about my future. I knew that with a good background in the sciences, I could get some kind of a job that I would enjoy as well as enable me to make some kind of a contribution to society and eat at least three times a day.

I never signed up for another music course. The Lincoln College Men fulfilled their responsibility to the school and to the community and continued to enjoy the association with each other, but we all began to realize that after college there would be no place for us as a group. Believe me, there were some difficult decisions to be made.

We acquired another music teacher at college our last year, a Mr. Laughlin, who had experience in the chorus of an opera company, and who taught us more about singing in an hour than some of the others did in a semester. He groomed us pretty fine, and promptly took us to Chicago to cut two records. We could not afford to publish the recordings and neither could the college. The masters were stored in the college library until money could be available for publication. That day never came, and our recordings were gone forever. The library, a part of the Administration building, burned.

My class load was more confining, especially the second semester, when I had more chemistry (qualitative and quantitative analysis) and in biology, vertebrate zoology. These courses had laboratory periods, of course, which were like going to heaven for me but were very time consuming.

I also had that English requirement that I had postponed as long as I could. Fortunately, the course was taught by a lady who was popular with the students and amazed me with her ability to turn what to me was the dullest of the dull subject matter into pertinent and interesting literary and communicative skills.

There was only one way out for me, and I soon found it: *master every lesson every day*. It sounds great as I sit here and type it, but believe me, it is impossible to do. At least as well as I would have liked. In spite of slacking off once in a while, I passed all of my courses and was ready to come back for more.

The first semester of 1936 was blessed with a long spell of sub-zero weather, creating a problem for those of us that commuted and for some of the students and faculty that lived in college-owned houses which had seen better days and could not be kept comfortable.

One afternoon, I went to the men's dorm (usually referred to as "the barn") to visit with some of my friends that lived there. We were pretty chilly, and wore jackets while we visited, solving all of the world's problems and wishing that someone would listen to us. Now, sixty-five years later, I know that young people are still trying to solve the world's problems and wondering what is the reason that the old folks have not made more progress in solving them. To the new generation, the problems are new. To the old generation, the problems are recognized as old friends (or enemies) and they know they are here to stay. They may wear a different hat, but the problems are still here. Arthur Gard, Edgar Monke and Byers Young, are you with me, still?

When I left the barn, I thought that I would take a turn past the place where Joy and Sue were rooming. It was a two-story house that served as a parsonage for a Methodist preacher. The girls had a room upstairs, unheated, and the downstairs rooms were nearly as cold. The minister had two or three little country churches to serve, but his congregations were too poor to support him. I am sure that some of his church members were cold, too. Joy and Sue were dressed for outdoors and were still cold. I took them home with me so that they could be warm, and, of course, "farm-fed."

I don't know how some of the others made out, but, as to be expected, it warmed up and life returned to normal. Whatever *that* is. They were not the only students to be hungry and cold, but I don't recall that anyone left school or became incurably ill from that cold spell.

Maurice emptying bundle rack at threshing machine

Harry Jackson and brother-in-law Maurice Lalicker showing off their new "Texas" hats

Clint, Corda, and Verna Mae Frye. Corda Lalicker Frye was a sister of Maurice's father "Chant." They were our nearest neighbors in Texas.

My wife, Joy Jackson and our son, Kenneth

Joy, Harry, and Kenneth Keith in Lincoln, Illinois

Elm Grove School, Dewitt County

The Harmony Four Male Quartet. Seated: Harold Arthur (L), El Masterson (R). Standing: Wayne Arthur (L), Harry Jackson (R).

Monica Joy Boatman Jackson

Central Park. Harry Owen, Pharmacist Mate 3rd Class, and son, Kenneth.

Joy Jackson and son, Kenneth Keith

Kenneth Lloyd Cecil, son of Herbert and Clarice Jackson Cecil

Harry and Joy's son, Kenneth, and wife, Judith Ann

Kenneth and wife Bernice Cecil, with Kenny Keith in St. Albans, New York

Faculty of Central School at Lincoln, Illinois

Harry Owen helps granddaughter Candace Leigh in milking a cow

Dolores Jackson's eightieth birthday party. Standing, left to right: Dale Braughton, Kenneth L. Cecil, Harry Lee Jackson, Clarice Jones, Kenneth Keith Jackson, Kenneth's daughter Candace, Ann Jackson, and Ethyl Cecil. Seated: Lee M. Jackson, Harry O. Jackson, Dolores L. Jackson, and Doris Braughton.

Clarice Jones and Jim Van Scyoc

Judy Jackson feeding the birds at Rocky Mountain National Park

XIT office in Channing, Texas. Formerly the head office, now a museum of one of the world's most famous ranches, the XIT.

Main Street in Channing, Texas. Building furthest left is the 1914–1921 Mercantile of Horn and Allen.

Middle Well Church in Moore County, Texas

Dolores' family

Harry and second wife, Dolores

Summer in Michigan

One day while visiting with Mr. Olson, he suggested that I might like to go with him to Michigan for the summer, not to work for pay, but to be introduced in a small way to actual botanical field work. Before he had finished speaking, I was fired up to go. I did have to check with Dad and Lee before I made a final commitment, I knew that I would be needed on the farm, and that if I went away, it would mean that more of the burden had to be shifted to them. They agreed to get along without me, except that I would have to come home in time to help with the threshing.

Irving agreed to that plan, except that he might not be finished with his work that early and, if so, he could not make the trip back to Lincoln to bring me home, I would have to take care of that myself. I had never hitch-hiked any place except one time when Ed Monke and I went to St. Louis. We were lucky on that trip. We got rides when we needed them, and enjoyed visiting with new people who picked us up. I believed that if I had to, I could hitch-hike home when the time came.

Joy thought that it would be an excellent experience for me as it was for her the summer before, except that I would have no pay. That was not a problem as we had enough money for groceries and our work was all of the recreation that we needed. Mrs. Olson did not go with us, electing to stay in Illinois. I am not sure, but I believe that she spent much of the time with some relatives.

Finally, the great day came and we headed north. Chicago was not strange to me, but I had never been further north than that. We went directly to Evanston and the Northwestern campus, where we planned to stay a couple of days. Irving spent time with Dr. Waterman and I worked in one of the laboratories preparing chemicals and selecting glassware and other materials that would be needed later.

We stayed at Lindgren House and ate at The Grill. I was impressed with the Northwestern campus and marvelled at the difference between it and the campus at Lincoln College. We met only a few people, most of them students, but they seemed to be pretty much the same type of young people that we had at home.

One thing was vastly different: It was a very stormy afternoon and night, and I could look out the window and see Lake Michigan in all her stormy glory. How different from Sugar Creek in Logan County! I have seen the lake many times since then, but never as wild as it was that night. There are enough vessels resting on the bottom of the lake to support the view of many that the Great Lakes are equal, if not superior, to any of the oceans as dangerous to ships in a storm.

I have not been on the Northwestern campus since that time, and I wonder if there are many people that remember the way it was then. I hope so.

The next morning, we went to the A&P grocery store. I had never been in a grocery store that large, and there were foods there that I had never heard of. We didn't buy those. What we did buy were staples; things that even I could prepare, and basket after basket of canned ready-to-eat things like pork and beans. Especially pork and beans.

Olson's car was one of the first Fords with the v-8 engine. All of our clothing and other gear was in the trunk in remembrance of the clothing that had been stolen the preceding summer. We loaded our purchases in back of the front seat—the heavy canned goods on the floor; the lighter materials on top. Clear to the top of the car and to the rearview window, it was the most completely loaded car in Evanston. Our total bill at the store? Ten dollars and forty-five cents.

Benzie County is fabulously beautiful, or at least it was in 1936. It probably is more so now due to the Betsie State Forest and other features that have been developed over the years. Crystal Lake, the Betsie River and the nearness to Lake Michigan create an environment that should satisfy almost anyone. It certainly did me.

We found Dr. Waterman's Red Cottage just the way the Olsons had left it last summer, just waiting for us to move in.

It didn't take long for us to settle in and get acquainted with the immediate area, including little Crystalia, which at that time was mostly a small post office.

Joy had forgotten to tell me about the post office. The mail was usually passed out by one or the other of the postmaster's daughters, pretty as pictures and with eyes approaching purple. The only eyes like that that I ever have seen. They were very early teens—probably a good thing.

When the Watermans arrived, I and Irving helped them get settled, and I liked them very much, although I rarely was with them.

One day, Irving, Dr. Waterman, and Mrs. Waterman were in a garage-like building looking over some equipment. On the floor, turned upside down (the way it should have been) was a canoe. Now, this was not *just* a canoe. It was an eighteen-foot Old Town, something that I had always wanted to get my hands on. I never dared to dream at that time that I would ever own one.

I guess that Mrs. Waterman read the expression on my face, but she never said a word.

A few days later, Dr. Waterman asked if I would help him and Irving haul the canoe to Crystal Lake. Well, of course I would. This exercise supposedly was to test the canoe for leaks.

We put the canoe in the water and, as usual, when I see that done I recall Longfellow's *Song of Hiawatha* in which the Indian builds a canoe that "Floated on the water, like a Yellow leaf in Autumn." I was so stirred by getting to handle that craft, that I quoted those lines. They just came out without my giving it any real thought.

Mrs. Waterman looked at me and said, "Harry, can you paddle a canoe?"

I didn't know how to answer that. I had never been in a canoe in my life. However, I had dreamed about it for so long and had read about the different strokes effective in making the canoe do what you wanted it to do, even practicing the strokes with a stick, that I just said, "Yes, I believe I can paddle this one. May I try it?"

"Of course."

I picked up the paddle. It was a good six inches too long for comfort; Dr. Waterman was a six-footer. I pushed off in my best Hiawatha manner and settled on my knees just a little way behind the middle thwart. I used my best J-stroke (American Red Cross), drew a bead on a tree down the shore a way, then turned around and paddled back, all from one side. Then I turned around again, and did a repeat of the exercise, paddling from the other side.

I pulled up, stepped out, and said to Dr. Waterman, "She doesn't leak." I was excited; I was scared. I was not deluded into thinking that I might do as well under less optimum conditions, but this round I had won.

Mrs. Waterman was a victim of poliomyelitis, and had lost the use of one hand and arm, at least for paddling and playing the piano, which I was told she was very good at. She liked to go canoeing, and I took her for several short rides while I was living in the Red Cottage.

My life was pretty pleasant during those weeks in Michigan. I spent most of the time in the field with Irving, mapping, measuring and just plain digging out all of the information that we could get. I was fascinated by the bogs. They represented plant associations that I had not even dreamed about, or heard of, and here I was at a real-life bog (Bear Lake Bog) walking (very carefully) out onto the floating mat of leatherleaf (Chamaedaphne) and seeing the relationship with the wild orchids, sedges, tamarack and dozens of other species of plants. Needless to say, there was a good sample of animal species, too; such as frogs and mosquitoes.

All good things have to come to an end some time, and a letter from home alerted me to the fact that the threshing machine was ready and that they expected to begin the summer's run next week. That meant pack up and get home.

Packing up was not much of a problem. I wadded up my field clothes for the trash, luckily I found a salesman going to Chicago, said my good-byes, and headed out. The salesman luckily had business in Pontiac, which took me close enough to home that I easily made it in the same day I left Michigan.

I think that people were more likely to offer rides to hitchhikers then than they are now. It was still depression-oriented times, and a helping hand was more likely to be offered.

In spite of the good times that I had in the north (Michigan was "far north" to me at that stage in my life), it was good to be home again. However, there were some drastic adjustments to be made. Here is the way Lee phrased it in his biographical notes:

> My grandfather died in 1935 at the age of eighty-five. His farm was sold, and in the fall of 1936, we were without a farm. We were deeply concerned, for farms for rent were hard to get. Dad and I spent a lot

of time and drove many miles that Fall, following any and all leads we heard of, but to no avail. I got a job driving a truck at a limestone quarry. My job was to haul rock from the quarry to the rock crusher. The rock in this area, at a place called Rocky Ford, was rich in limestone and farmers spread it on their fields to sweeten the soil. That helped clover and other legumes which in turn fertilized the soil.

I was milking four cows and driving twelve miles to work. I had to be on the job at daylight. We worked until dark with an hour off for lunch. We worked in all kinds of weather and was paid thirty cents an hour.

I was glad to get any kind of work at any price. I came home one night and my wife told me that Dad and my brother had done the milking for me. I was glad to hear that, but she had even better news. Dad, that day, had rented an even bigger farm in an adjoining county, and we would move the following March, the usual moving time. We were very happy. Our hopes had materialized and life took on a satisfied meaning.

Little did I know that I would farm that place for thirty-two years, but I did.

All of which put a new light on my homecoming. Of course, I dreaded leaving our old neighbors and the place that my great-grandfather had first carved out of the tall grass prairie, but I also knew that I would never live there myself, and if I was going to make a place for myself in the world, I had better be getting at it. First of all, of course, was the business at hand, harvest the crops and get back in the classroom. That was what I did.

Joy had gone home for the summer hoping to find work, but had to take a job in a fairly nice sandwich shop which paid about three dollars a week. Like Lee's rock hauling job, it was that or nothing.

Of course, the first time that I could get away, I went to Effingham to see her. It was at this time that we both felt that very probably, whatever we did in the future was almost sure to be done together. It is about a hundred miles from Lincoln to Effingham, and today, I would not even be willing to drive that old Whippet across town, much less take any kind of a trip in it. Of course, there were no traffic problems as we know them now, and four-lane interstate roads were not even a gleam in God's eye yet. So, with three or four dollars in my pocket, I made that trip and I certainly knew that it would not be the last. Over the years that I drove that little car, I had several experiences that now would scare me to death. One of note was a problem I had on my way home one Sunday evening: I had been cruising along at my usual cruising speed (forty miles per hour) when the engine stopped cold. I checked the battery posts first; they were OK and the battery was charged. Suddenly, I noticed that the wire from the coil was broken. I also found that it was too short to recouple.

I was well-equipped with tools to make repairs, a pair of pliers and a screwdriver. Also, luckily, my trusty pocket knife. I was also equipped with several years of experience in making emergency repairs on worn-out farm machinery.

Along the road, on the northbound lane, there was a beautiful barbed wire fence. I had built a good many fences, and I knew that frequently there was a piece at the end post that was just wound around the post a few times to finish it off. This fence had one, too. I cut it off, spliced it into the coil wire, and drove on home. The fence was not damaged at all.

I kept that car until the early summer of 1937 and it was still running on the barbed wire from the fence. That was the first of only two times that I have ever had to make repairs on a car at night, but for many years, I carried a piece of good clean baling wire along with my pliers and screwdriver.

The rest of the summer was spent doing the regular farm work that we were so accustomed to, but there was a real difference in the spirit with which we approached it, knowing that this was the final time that we would harvest those acres of land that we knew so well. It seemed that every swell and every swale, every rock (what few there were) and every bush had some kind of a story behind it; like the wild strawberry beds at the end of the row and the crab apple tree in the fence row that separated two eighty-acre tracts. That old tree never bore fruit, but a box trap placed under it in the winter was sure to provide several cottontail rabbits to eat or sell. Frequently, I sold the dressed rabbits to our grocer for twenty-five cents each. More frequently, they ended up on our own table.

Senior Year, Continued

I returned to college in the fall, and was eligible for graduation in January, but I elected to stay for the spring semester to pick up some credits that I thought would be helpful. They were subject-matter courses as well as some others in education and I enjoyed them. They helped me to have instruction in addition to the minimum requirements for certification.

In early March, we moved to the new farm. It was in DeWitt County, about fifteen miles east of Lincoln, and five miles south of Waynesville.

All of our farm equipment was loaded onto hay racks and box wagons to be moved. Lee and I each drove a team and wagon to the new farm on the morning of the third of March. It was, as usual for March, cold and damp. We both had on all of the heavy coats that we owned and still would have to get off the wagon and walk alongside it to keep warm. It was a long day, but when we finally arrived, that place surely looked mighty good to us. Eventually, everything was moved, and we all went through the regular routine of getting settled in our new home.

We liked it fine. It was a comfortable house with a basement, and for the first time since we left Texas, Mom had a sink in the kitchen.

Of course, I commuted to college as I had done before we moved. The roads were good gravel, and there was very little plant growth along the sides to make snow drifts except in one place.

Carl (Si) Sprague and his wife, Ruth, lived a half mile south of our place. They had three fine boys of grade school age and two girls in high school. On my way home from school, along the road in front of their house was three fine boys sitting on the grass. I stopped, we visited for several minutes, and that was as long as it took to develop a fast friendship that lasted as long as they lived, not only with the boys, but with the whole family.

One incident that happened the following winter will confirm the kind of relationship that we had. One winter night, I was coming home rather late. It had snowed, and a radiator-cap-drift had formed in this one likely place mentioned before . . . right in front of the Sprague home.

I banged as hard as the Whippet would go, hoping to break through to open road, but there was nothing doing. I was hopelessly stuck. Also, I didn't want to walk a half mile home in the snow which was about ten inches or so high.

A fine young man named Frank Gambrel was helping Si with the corn harvest, and I knew where his bedroom was, just at the head of the stairs on the second floor. I went in, left my hat and coat where Si and Ruth could see it in the morning, and climbed into bed with Frank. He didn't know that I was there until morning.

After breakfast, we pulled the car out with a tractor and I went on home. Lee and Dad had seen the car and knew where I was. They were not worried, knowing that I would be all right, no matter where I stayed.

Since that time, I was always reluctant to lock the house door at night. Unfortunately, our society has degenerated to the point that in some areas, you not only have to lock your doors, you have to have alarms and other forms of protection, too.

Well, I finally graduated from college, even if it was just a junior college. I earned every grade point that I got at Lincoln College. It was a fine little school, and I am proud to have been selected as an honor graduate at my fiftieth class reunion.

Post-College

After graduation, I got serious about finding a one-room school that needed a teacher. It was early in the year, but I wanted my name in the pot as soon as there was a vacancy. At that time, if a teacher was not going to be rehired, the board of directors (composed of three registered voters in the community) was to notify the teacher by the first day of April, so a few days prior to this date, I began my crusade by visiting with county superintendants. They would interview prospects, and, if asked by the school directors, would give members his evaluation. This was a great help to directors, as most of them knew very little about keeping a school operating smoothly and up-to-date. In fact, most of the ones I talked to wanted their school operated just like it had been when they were pupils.

On the other hand, the county superintendants freely provided the applicant with known vacancies and the names and locations of the board members. Without this help, we never would have found the board members.

Once I found the directors, I soon learned that it was better to catch them alone. If their wives were present, they asked most of the questions, or stated flat out what the teacher had to do. "Teach table manners" was the leading one. I applied for forty-one vacancies in the summer of 1937, and was not hired by any of them. "We don't think the pupils would like a man teacher," or "We might consider you if you were married."

Salaries ranged from sixty-five to eighty dollars per month. One evening, I got home late, parked Dad's car, (the Whippet had given up the ghost) and said, "To Hell with it."

Next, I went to the power company in Lincoln. I was not a stranger to any of the administrators there, and I knew that I would not get a run-around. I didn't. Flat out, the manager said, "Harry, the only vacancy that I have is for a line man. You would make a good one, but if you start at that, it is as far as you will go. I won't hire you." He also said, "Keep on hunting, one of these days you will get a surprise."

My "surprise" was a chance to sell Hoover vacuum cleaners door to door. I decided to try it.

I was selected to go to Jacksonville for practice in their sales method, and after a couple of days, I would be assigned an area to work.

I had to have transportation, as I had to spend all week in Jacksonville. I couldn't commute. So, I shopped around and finally selected a 1930 model Chevrolet coupe in green with no brakes to speak of. Twenty dollars down and ten dollars a month. Total cost less interest, was one hundred eighty-seven dollars and fifty cents. I drove her home, replaced the brake bands, and gave her a bath. I drove that little coupe for several years and wish I had it now.

I paid attention to the instructions that I got about selling Hoovers. I knew that they were a good product and I had no qualms about urging sales to most people.

What I didn't like was that I was assigned to one of the poorest sections of town. Some of the homes I visited did not have a carpet or a drape in the place. They were poor people but I could have talked them into paying their ten dollars down and owning the cheaper model. I knew that if I did that, they probably were going to have to skimp on bread. I didn't push.

After two days, on Friday, I had not sold a single cleaner and I was sure that I never would have unless someone really needed one. I was a lousy salesman then, and I still am.

I went home, made myself available for farm work, and got more than I needed. The wages, if you ate lunch (we still called it dinner) at home, were two dollars and fifty cents a day. A day was from about seven in the morning until six in the afternoon. We had supper when I got home, usually around seven. I just worked when and where I was needed, if I could be spared from helping Dad and Lee. I was not planning on shucking corn in the fall as the plan was to have it harvested with a machine.

All in all, the future just didn't look too bright. As sometimes happens, you just might get a break. One of the families that lived near us had a child that had been crippled by polio. He could not attend regular school, and the district is required by law to provide a teacher for him. I was available. It paid forty dollars a month for eight months.

Little Warren was a great kid. He wasn't too keen on learning, but he did fairly well and I enjoyed working with him. Four hours a day at forty dollars for twenty days is about fifty cents an hour, disregarding holidays, etc. That was pretty good and I saved a little money—but not much.

The employment that I had was, in many ways, enjoyable. The long haul was little better than a meal ticket. It seemed to be so little after the hard work and expense of college that at times I felt a twinge of depression, wondering if there would be other opportunities, and, if there were, would I recognize them. I had a wonderful relationship with my family, but there was something missing. I suspected that it was Joy, but there didn't seem to be anything that I could do about that because I just didn't think that I had a very good chance of being able to support a wife.

Joy was spending the summer with her folks. They were living in Effingham, trying to eke out a living any way that they could. Joy's father had lost nearly all of his sight, and had spent their savings trying to save it. Now, they were destitute.

One day I got a letter from Joy (not unusual) saying, in effect, "Come."

So, the following weekend, I went to see her. We had a pleasant time as her folks were always nice to me and had long before resigned to the fact that I would someday be their son-in-law. It didn't take long to see that they were in deep trouble. Joy and I had a pretty long conference, and after considering as many aspects of the problem as we could, decided that we would get married. We would certainly have as much together as we had separately. Further debate would not help, and the Easter season was a good any time.

We made our plans as best we could, with so many people around, but after a couple of short walks down to the woods and back, we were certain that the plans that we had made were the best that we could do, under the circumstances, some of which were rather indefinite as you will see.

Even today, I find that there are little details that I had forgotten completely or that were a little hazy after sixty-five years. To be certain that I have the facts stated correctly, I am going to quote directly from Joy's account as written in her Bride's Book under the heading, "Personal Notes About Our Honeymoon." (I am sure we will be forgiven if the notes are not *too* personal.)

I was to have met Harry in Mattoon, Illinois, on the eleven o'clock bus, supposedly to visit his folks and *viceversa*. I had bought my ticket on Wednesday, April 13 and had not enquired about the bus, since it had not been that long since I had taken the same bus to meet Harry in Decatur. So, I was much annoyed when, at 10:15, the bus had not come in. I then said to Mama, who was visiting with me, "I believe that that bus only comes in at 10:10 on certain days of the week."

Upon inquiring, we were told that the bus had changed time and would not leave until 10:38. I was sure that Harry would worry, so I telephoned for him to come on down for me. However, he did not receive the message until 1:30. He left Mattoon immediately, arriving down home about 2:30. At 3:00, we left for St. Louis.

The wind was very strong and we were on old route 40 making very poor time. We got through St. Louis just before dark, decided that we were "up a stump" and stopped at a filling station to tell the man what we wanted to do. He directed us to Clayton as our best choice, and we arrived there about 7:30.

A caretaker of the courthouse and county jail combined was so very good to us, calling on two Justices (of the peace) numerous times without success. Finally, about 8:45, he said, "We have one more chance. George Hart, the famous marrying justice." Mr. Charles Luey called the judge while we were getting a bite to eat. Harry and I and the Judge arrived at the courthouse at the same time, and at 9:30, we left in the Judge's Chrysler Imperial for St. Louis for our license. From there we went to St. Charles to the judge's marriage chapel, where we were married.

The chapel was a lovely little place with nice furniture and palms around the pulpit. After the I do's, the judge took us back to Clayton as he was en route to three other couples who were to apply for licenses yet that night. It was 11:20 as we went for our bags and chatted again with our friend Mr. Luey, who had been watching for us.

We had a very nice room at the Claymore at Clayton. On Friday, we had breakfast and were ready to leave for St. Louis at 8:30, headed for Forest Park. We spent the entire day there except for going up town for lunch. Oh! That bean soup! It was the best that I ever hope to taste!

On the way home, we stopped at Cahokia Mound State Park. That was the first time that either of us had seen the mound. In fact, I am not sure that I even knew about it's importance until we visited there. On the way home, we stopped in Broadwell to see my (now *our*) dear friend, Boyd Read. He was flattered to be the first of the young friends to hear the news. We decided to stop and spend the night with my sister, Frances, and brother-in-law, Maurice Lalicker. My little niece, Marcellen, said several times to Joy, "That sure is a pretty ring you're wearing!" Neither Maurice or Francis caught on. Finally, Francis said, "I wish you two would get married so it wouldn't be so much trouble to fix beds." When we told her that we were married, we had to show them the certificate to make them believe it.

We all went to church the next morning and Frances had a chance to sneak the information to my mother before we got home. The rest of the family didn't know until my sister Clarice noticed Joy's ring.

Joy was very happy that the family approved of her and of the way that we had planned the wedding. She writes in her Bride's Book:

> There weren't many tears, and I am so happy. I feel as if I couldn't stand it if everyone hadn't been so glad for us. I feel I'm the luckiest bride ever. If anyone had objected to our marriage, I don't know who it was.

On Monday night, there was the expected "Chivari." We were not expecting it to be so soon! It was a complete surprise, the result of a lot of devious behavior on the part of Clarice and her husband, J. A. (Rusty) Jones. I took an involuntary bath in the horse tank, but the party was a great success.

Finding a Home

We had to sponge off my folks for a while, but that was not all bad because I could help out with the farm work and still be making arrangements for a home of our own.

DeWitt County is, like Logan County, a part of Illinois that was fashioned into rich farmland by the millenia that had been tall grass prairie after a somewhat respectful treatment by the Wisconsin continental ice-sheet. Consequently, it could be, and was, laid off in nicely ordered sections of land and country roads.

On the gravel road that ran north and south a mile east of what was now the home farm, lived a fine couple whom I had always liked very much, Carter and Anna Sprague. Their house and outbuildings were set back from the road a little distance and a little house, probably built as a tenant house for a hired man and his wife, was directly on the road.

One day when I was helping Carter with some field work, I noticed the little house. I took a good look at it because it was so nicely painted and homey looking.

I didn't think much about it after that, until the last few weeks before Joy and I were married.

I didn't say anything to Joy about it until I had a better look and had talked to Mr. Sprague about renting or buying the house and enough land to at least have a garden and a few fruit trees. It had been neglected for several years, the roof leaked and it needed plaster and paint. Lots of it.

Carter said, "Harry, I would be glad to rent the place to you and Joy, but it just isn't fit to live in."

"I can make it fit to live in if you will give me credit on the rent for what cash I have to spend on it."

"How about the labor?"

"I'll donate the labor. How much rent do you want?"

"Would five dollars a month be too much?"

Never would I have dreamed about renting a house for five dollars a month. On the other hand, there was no indoor plumbing or water. In fact, the only water was from a cistern and was only used for laundry. We had to haul water for drinking and cooking. There was a good outdoor toilet about a hundred feet from the house, and another little storage building just outside the kitchen door, but no electricity. It stood on a plot of land at least as big as two city lots.

Joy approved, and we went to work. We needed wood shingles for the roof. (You could look up through the living room ceiling and see the north star.) There was no use to do anything else until the roof was repaired. It took nearly an entire bundle of cedar shingles, laid four inches to the weather.

I had never plastered before, but I had seen it done. I did a fair job, I guess. At least nobody complained.

There were four rooms, two in front and two in the back. In front, the north room was the bedroom, the south room was the living room. The kitchen took up the south half of the west area and the other little room had no use at all for several weeks.

Joy went to the county seat and bought a few rolls of wall paper. She was good at applying it and finished before I was done with the painting in the unpapered rooms.

Floor coverings were limited to ready-cut linoleum, which could be bought for from three to five dollars each and were not expected to last a life time.

This first summer, we learned how to be scavengers. We rescued a two-burner kerosene stove that had been used by Lee and Bessie. It had two chimneys with wicks at the bottom that could be adjusted to have the size of flame desired. They did a good job of cooking, if you didn't expect too much. The legs for the stove were missing, so we set the stove on two wood orange crates standing on end. We had picked up several of these orange crates from our favorite grocery man and they served well as cupboards and storage bins for many months. I still have three or four of them, serving the same purpose in my basement, except that now they are antiques. A portable oven could be set above one burner. The one that we had made very acceptable biscuits when operated by an excellent cook, which I had.

We used a card table until I got a more appropriate one built, eating in the kitchen.

Joy found a love seat and a large chair in a second-hand store trash pile. They were a matched pair, heavy oak with lion faces carved on the end of the arms and lion feet on the end of the legs. They were a mess, dirty and stained. They had at one time been upholstered, but all of the cover was missing. I couldn't see any use for them except possibly for firewood.

Fortunately, I kept my mouth shut, because I recognized the quality of the original workmanship. Seeing such a fine set in the sad state that this one was in was, to Joy, like waving a red flag in front of a Mexican bull. Eventually, a beautiful rubbed down, refinished, and reupholstered set graced our living room.

I found out, years after we had parted with it, that antique dealers would have given a comparatively tidy sum for it.

We didn't realize how many close friends we had until ladies from our old home neighborhood as well as those from our new neighborhood started giving "showers" for Joy. Our little house was crammed in every nook and cranny with wonderful gifts for the new bride and groom. Cooking utensils, bedding, housewares . . . you name it, the new Jacksons had it.

I knew that as long as I lived, I would never be able to adequately express my appreciation to those friends who did so much for us.

That little house was not fancy. It did not have sheeting outside on the wall studs; just the drop siding on the outside, and the plaster on the inside. It was cross-ventilated so that in summer, it was nice and cool, but in the winter, it was impossible to heat comfortably. We just piled on more covers in the winter and wore long johns about six months out of the year.

This was truly the beginning of an era in our lives. It was no longer Joy or frequently, Harry, but a new association. References to us now were Joy and Harry, or Harry and Joy. Where you found one, you found the other nearby. Always. For forty years.

Work Woes

We did have one little problem. Winter was someplace down the road and there was not going to be my regular sustaining farm work to fall back on for groceries and warmth. I have always been well fed and warm, and I had no intention to slack off on either of these physical conditions.

We both knew that we could get jobs as clerks in a store, but that would have to be a last resort as neither of us really enjoyed selling. Not at twenty-five cents an hour.

Soon, it became obvious that I had better be doing something. I had a wife to support, and that was a privilege the I was not going to relinquish. Of course, the first consideration was a big vegetable garden. We planted a little of anything that would grow in central Illinois. That was about anything that would grow anyplace.

If you look around a bit, you can nearly always find elderly or disabled people who have fruit trees, but are not physically able to harvest their produce. We found several perfectly healthy people who just had no use for so much fruit, mostly peaches and cherries, but later apples, too. We picked and canned. Quart after quart of beautiful fruit in Mason jars, racked on the shelf so that guests could see how industrious we were. We had chickens that supplied eggs galore. We did not have fried chicken. At least, not very often. I have never been willing to kill and eat animals that I produced and cared for and that trusted me. We thought we were doing OK, and as it turned out, we were.

Just about the time we started harvesting the crops that we were so proud of, I found out that the teacher of the Elm Grove school had resigned. I lost no time in applying for the position and was hired. Eighty dollars a month for the eight month term. We were rich! Of course, we had to deduct a few dollars for the pension plan and medical insurance. From eighty dollars, it hurt. I had a hard time thinking about retirement when I hadn't even started!

I had a nice building, a dependable furnace, and well-kept furniture and other equipment considered essential to a one-room country school. It was just a mile and a half from our house, an easy walk when the car wouldn't start. That was an ever-present possibility, especially in the winter, after you lack electricity to operate a battery charger.

I had ten or twelve pupils, all of them neatly dressed and well-behaved, and I liked them all right from the start.

I have already offered a general description and included most of the problems and rewards associated with this great American tradition. Sitting on the other side of the desk didn't change the over-all picture very much. About all I can say is that I experienced all that I wrote about from both points of view; that of the pupil, and that of the teacher. I have never been a member of a school board, thank God!

How about the old saying: Some (of both pupils and parents) will like you; some will not. Believe me, it is true. And in varying degrees. Here is an example: During the late summer, Joy got a letter from her mother that left her worried about her mother's health. It was a busy time on the farm where her folks were living and Joy elected to go help her mother with the canning or whatever it was that they were doing.

Promptly, one of the parents in the school district drove over most of the neighborhood telling people that Joy had left me, and probably more that I never heard about.

Well, the word got around, all right, but the blame was put where it belonged. I didn't hear anything about it until months later.

It was at this time that the schools were being consolidated, and for all practical purposes, the one-room country school was no more. There were many factors to be considered, but in view of the changing times, there was no other choice.

For better or worse, I was out of it. Or, at least I thought I was, until they decided to keep our home district school open one more year, keeping me on the "one room school" circuit for one more year.

By the spring of 1940, I knew that there was no future in teaching with the amount of education that I had. School administrators and boards of directors were not going to consider teachers with or without a valid license and years of experience, without at least a baccalaureate (bachelor's) degree.

I had already accumulated enough of a background in the physical and biological sciences to at least have some idea of what they were about. I knew nothing about the earth sciences, so I began to enquire about courses available and possibly a good school or instructor that could help me fill in the gap.

Eventually, I came up with both the school and the instructor; Dr. Norman Newell at the University of Wisconsin.

I wrote to the University, was accepted, and arranged for living quarters. The "living quarters" consisted of a wood platform at the University's Campground on the shore of beautiful Lake Mendota, just a short drive from the campus.

We bought a "Baker" tent, a couple of camp cots, a Coleman gasoline lantern and a two-burner Coleman camp stove. We had enough camping experience to be adequately prepared with bedding and clothes. We finally decided that we were ready, except for some odds and ends; writing materials, notebooks stamps for letters home, and most important of all, every penny of money that we could dig up: a little over one hundred dollars.

We were in the store that handled school supplies, making these last purchases, when one of the owners saw me looking at a typewriter. He said, "Harry, you need to take that to Wisconsin."

I said, "I know I do, but we can't afford it."

We passed a few more remarks, finished our other purchases, and went to the cash register to pay our bill.

"How would you like to take that typewriter with you, and next fall, pay me ten dollars each payday."

I couldn't refuse. There were no interest charges and no contract of any kind other than a handshake and wishes for a good summer. Trummels, in Clinton, the county seat of DeWitt County. Friends, indeed.

When we reached Madison, we drove to the campground, pitched our tent, and the next day, I went to the campus to register. I had reservations about being able to deal with big university courses, and was anxious to put them to rest. We were sure that it would be different from Lincoln College.

I reported in, paid my platform rent, and went to see the instructor to register. At that time, you registered with the professor.

Dr. Newell was a young man, a most likeable person who made you feel at home at once. His lectures were fascinating, the subject matter intensely interesting to me and the lab work and field trips (Joy got to go on the field trips with me) were valuable experiences. This course stands at the top of my "value scale" of college-level courses that I have ever taken, and it was a great privilege to have studied geology under his guidance.

One more item: There were in our class, two young women who looked and acted as if there should always be someone around to do their bidding. I took copious notes at the lectures, and frequently, the girls would ask if they could borrow them. I didn't really object to that as they took good care of them and always returned them promptly. Of course, they were typed up each day.

One day, Dr. Newell stopped me after class, and said, "Harry, typed notes around here sell for thirty cents a sheet for carbon copies, and they can afford it!"

Believe me when I say I took notes. If the professor sneezed, if there had been a way to record it, I would have done so. I sold enough notes that summer to pay for this typewriter, which cost ninety dollars. Mr. Trummel got his money, too.

We didn't live very "high on the hog" that six-week period, but we didn't go hungry, either.

Many years later, when our son graduated with high honors from Illinois State University at Normal, Illinois, I had received a note from Dr. Newell asking if that might be my son. He had seen the list of honor students in print and remembered Joy and me.

After classes ended, we broke camp and headed for home, hoping to make the trip by noon the next day. We almost made it, but not quite.

We were cruising along, relaxed and comfortable, a few miles south of Janesville, when the little Chevy started missing. I slowed down and studied the situation, wondering if we could make it to some kind of repair shop without ruining something.

Well, night is not a good time to hunt for repair shops. I had decided what we had was a broken valve spring, and all I would need was someone to sell me a spring. We finally found an auto parts store which was a part of a service station complex. It was still open and had a spring, but no one to make the repair. That was all right, I didn't want to spend the money anyway. Down the road a few miles, we found a place to pull off the highway by driving into a corn field. Joy held a flashlight; I replaced the spring, and we finally made it home—just in time to get ready to leave to drive my father and mother to Oklahoma to visit with Mom's sister (Aunt Naome) and her family.

Dad had traded their little Model A ford for a 1935 Plymouth. It was a comfortable car to ride in and pleasant to drive. Our cruising speed was forty-five miles per hour, which was about as fast as the roads would allow. Of course, we took Route 66 west across Missouri and into Oklahoma and on to Sulfur toward Aunt Naome and her family: Hazel, Millie and Lucille.

Route 66 was only partially paved, but had been improved somewhat from what it was in the 1930s. Some of it had a one-car width (probably nine feet) paved with bricks down the middle of the road bed. When two cars met, each car was to keep the two wheels on the driver's side on the bricks, and the two wheels on the passenger side could do their best to keep up with the wheels on the pavement, unless the ruts were too deep and pulled you over into the ditch. This is no joke, although it has all the ear-marks of a very bad one.

We enjoyed our stay there immensely. I hadn't seen Millie or Hazel since I was a little kid, but Lucille, who was a deaf mute, had visited us in Illinois with her mother. They, especially Lucile, liked Joy very much which pleased me. Joy learned to communicate with Lucile very quickly, and we both enjoyed seeing Platte National Park and the giant artesian springs, swimming in the large pool, and visiting the "roots" of the very old mountain range which, except for the slanting beds of rock which are barely above the ground, have eroded to form a peneplane.

This was a great trip for all of us. Dad and Mom enjoyed every minute in Oklahoma, but were also looking forward to seeing the old friends and neighbors in Texas. I was anxious to see the place where I was born and to verify some of the memories and impressions that after nearly twenty years just *might* not be quite like I thought they were.

We stayed with Clyde and Helen Messenger and their children, who could be relied upon to give you all the news related to people they all knew, a trip to Channing, and finally, to the old farmstead that was just the way I remembered it. Even I was surprised that when I would see a given room, I could relate it to the memory of something that had happened there.

We took a more northerly route home, coming through a part of Oklahoma I had not seen, then part of Kansas, and on home on Route 54.

There was only one "tragedy." We stopped for a meal at Louisiana, Missouri. I hung my hat on a rack just inside the door, and when we left, I walked right past my hat and didn't even miss it until we were nearly home. I think I probably won't ever go back for it. I have another one now.

When the home district school closed, I was officially unemployed. Again.

This time, I decided that I had had enough, and my teaching career had ended. I had enjoyed my year at Central and was reluctant to begin a search for some other kind of work. There was no other choice, as there were no other one-room schools open and larger schools had either hired the misplaced teachers or were hiring only those with Bachelor's or more advanced degrees.

I was in no hurry to find new employment, partly because it would mean moving from friends and family, and I was reluctant to leave either of them. It was a busy time for farmers, and I had discovered that someone who could come in and work for a few days or weeks, just to get through a seasonal demand, was the choice of many farmers because they did not have to pay for the slack time. Also, I could get a little extra pay by living at home and commuting. It worked very well for me.

Early in the summer, I was working for a neighbor, I believe that I was cultivating corn. I had taken a sandwich for lunch, and didn't get home until evening.

One day, I got home at the usual time, and when I walked into the house, I could see that something was terribly wrong. Joy was almost shaking, was white-faced like she was about to faint, and I could see that she had been crying. She had, indeed, had a harrowing experience.

She had just stepped out the kitchen door into the yard when she heard a loud call, the kind that is made when someone is in deep trouble. The call finally became, "HELP!" and Joy recognized the call as coming from Mr. Sprague. She ran as fast as she could go over to their driveway, and toward the house. She found Carter in a pen where he kept some of his hogs and a large boar. Apparently, he had carried a basket of corn to feed them, but his feet had slipped off the board fence, and he had fallen into the pen with the boar. No one knew for sure how it had happened, as Carter didn't remember and Joy found him in the pen being attacked by the boar. Joy saw the blood and helped Carter to get out of the pen, but she could not remember how she had distracted the boar, or how she had got him out of the pen.

Carter had a bad tear through the skin of his thigh and another up the right side of his back. Joy ran to the house, grabbed a sheet off the bed and did the best she could to stop the bleeding.

I had driven our car to work, but Carter had a late model Chevrolet, so Joy helped him get as comfortable as she could and took him to the hospital in Clinton. She had just gotten home a few minutes before I did, and she was still upset. Mrs. Sprague had been away from home, and I don't know how she was notified. Carter recovered completely, but we never again could make him take a penny for house rent as long as we lived there.

Late summer had always been my favorite season, but it is usually a busy time. The corn, of course, had been "laid by" in late June. The wheat and oats had been shocked, and was ready for threshing, that great time when neighbors pooled their resources, not the least of which was the spirit of friendship and cooperation.

I had always helped with the threshing, and expected to this year. It was something of a surprise to me to find that most of the farmers were not going to thresh, but were going to combine their crops, eliminating the need for shocking the grain then spending extra days going around the neighborhood to thresh.

It was a lucky break for me to know that one man wanted to thresh because he wanted a straw stack to provide shelter and some roughage for his cattle. But he would not thresh unless he could get me to build his straw stack. He could, and I did. When we finished the job, I got down, helped clean the separator for storage, tried to hide my true feelings from the other men, and never operated a threshing machine again.

I think Joy was beginning to feel that I had better be doing something about a job for the winter months. We had both agreed that my chances for a teaching job was very limited and I didn't care. I had enough of being the "last" of something, like one-room schools and threshing machines.

On the other hand, I knew that I might have to take any job that I could get. Most people seemed to feel that the Depression was over, but that was true only in somebody's magazine article, not in the real world. I was still getting day work, but that would not last long.

One day, I was offered a short job at the local grain elevator. There were several farmers that used anthracite (hard coal) for heating their houses in winter. Our local mines produced only soft coal, so the anthracite had to be shipped by rail in box cars to Tabor elevator, scooped into a truck, delivered to the customer, and scooped again into the customer's coal shed. The next day, I stood on the truck bed, looking through the box car door at forty-one tons of coal to be delivered. Three dollars a day. The car could remain on the siding for three days. If it took longer than that to unload, there was a three dollar per day rent fee to be charged to the elevator. The elevator did not want to pay the rent fee, so that meant I was expected to deliver forty-one tons of coal in three days. Total scooping weight, eighty-two tons.

I tried, but I couldn't do it. Joy's folks had moved up north and were living nearby, so I got her father to help me, and we got the job done. That was one of the times that I wished that I weighed a hundred and sixty pounds instead of my regular hundred and twenty.

I had barely recuperated from the coal-hauling when the manager decided to have me help the regular, full-time man with some routine odd jobs. The man's name was Frank Witt, and we enjoyed working together.

Saturdays were usually "clean up/odd jobs" day, which made it possible to quit early, get home, and get ready to go to town for the necessary shopping. Farmers were frequently late, so the stores stayed open until ten o'clock.

It so happened, though, that on this particular Saturday, we got a call: the Smith (not their real names) sisters were low on chicken feed and needed two bags today.

Frank and I filled two burlap bags (one hundred pounds each) and put them on the truck.

Frank said, "You take these, and when you come back, go on home, I'll finish up here."

That sounded like a good deal to me, so I went to the customer's house, and asked them where to put the feed.

"Bring it here," one said, "I'll show you where to put it."

I was parked at the gate to the front lawn. There was a good hundred feet to the porch, then five or six steps up onto the porch, into the dining room, up a flight of stairs to the second floor, then up another flight of stairs to the attic. Two bags. Two trips. Two hundred pounds. A hot summer day. Late for supper. Worried wife.

The seventh day God rested. So did I.

A New Job

I "loafed" at home for two or three days, worked a little on the Chevy coupe, determined that it was rusted out so badly that I had better start looking for a replacement, and wondered what had happened to the price of used cars. I was determined to have power-assisted brakes on all four wheels, something that I had never had. The replacement was closer than I knew.

The next Sunday afternoon, Joy and I had been playing badminton in the front yard when a strange car pulled into the drive. There were two men in it, and they wanted to know if I was Harry Jackson. I said that I was and they introduced themselves and said that they were Keith Roberts and Mr. Heinle.

They were board members of the grade school at Argenta, and they were in need of a man to teach the seventh and eighth grades, be the principal of the three teacher school, and help the boys with the basketball program. Was I available?

Well, I was surely available. They made it plain that I would have to meet with the other board member, a Mr. Lukenbill, and that they were certain that I would want to know more about the school, see the building, and perhaps move to Argenta far enough from the beginning of the term to check the supplies and do whatever planning seemed necessary.

I introduced Joy to them and we set a date to meet. They said that they hoped that I would be satisfied with the arrangements, and left.

We liked everything that we saw. The building was nice, the few people we met were friendly and the house available to rent was very satisfactory. We could move anytime that was convenient.

Moving was no problem. Lee's pick-up held nearly all or our household pieces and the car held all of our clothing. As I look back upon those times, I wonder how we lived.

Hundreds of times, I have heard now-affluent people say, "We didn't know we were poor." I think I know how they feel now and how they felt then, but as for Joy and me, I can truthfully say that we darned well knew that we were poor. What we did not know was that we were destitute. Or, at least, that we had been, but that our economic situation was, at last, improving.

I found that I had two really fine teachers; Maythel Fairweather for the middle-graders and Rose Gisinger for the little folks. I cannot thank them enough for the help that they gave me getting the term underway, and all through the year. At that time, I was completely happy and wouldn't have traded jobs with anyone.

The pupils were intelligent, friendly, cooperative, and a pleasure to teach . . . to a point. The point took me completely by surprise.

Basketball season was expected to start . . . now! I had reservations about the basketball season and how to handle the situation, but I felt that we were being pushed a little too far. I soon learned that basketball was dominant.

We had the high school gymnasium reserved for our use after school one day per week for about two hours. Fine. I had expected some intramural games, perhaps some with nearby schools. What I had was a team capable of winning the county tournament. It *would* win. Or, at least, it had better!

Well, I would do the best I could, which was not very good. I did not like basketball (I hated football even more, but that was irrelevant). I not only hated it, but I did not like to coach, either. Not when we were up for big stakes like the county tournament. I had the idea that I was to give the boys a chance to polish up some of the fundamentals and give as many students as possible an opportunity to participate and sharpen up for high-school level competition.

I had some sharp players (three of them were board members' children). It was good that no one interfered with my plan, but several surely let it be known that next year there was going to be a coach. Worst of all, all of the kids knew how unpopular I had become.

Finally, it was all over. We had to be satisfied with second place in the tournament, the damage was done.

I had forty-two pupils in my room, and two grade levels. With a lower quality of pupil, it would have been impossible to maintain any kind of suitable grade-point average, but we did all right, and I was proud of my pupils even if they were not proud of their coach.

There was one country school in the county that was near (two miles, I was told) our school. Next term, there would be two pupils from that school that would have to be transported to our school. Would I be willing to get these children, then take them home after school? If so, they would pay me an extra thirty-five dollars. I said I would. I knew that it would be more convenient for me to do it than to get some town person.

The problem was that I thought they meant to pay thirty-five dollars a month. What they had meant was thirty-five dollars for the term. To this, I said, "No."

It didn't set well. I don't know who finally ended up hauling the poor little children.

This was also the term that included Pearl Harbor Day. When we went to school on Monday after the bombing of Pearl Harbor, I was amazed to find that some of the pupils didn't even know that we had been attacked.

I devoted most of the morning to acquainting them with some of the salient facts and history of the whole business. Perhaps I overrated the need for twelve to fourteen-year-olds to have a little knowledge of what was going on and was definitely going to affect the lives of every one of us—including me.

There was only a lukewarm acceptance from the pupils, except for a few of the really bright ones.

One day in early spring, one of the board members told me that they had an opportunity to hire a well-thought-of young man who was a good coach and who would transport the children. My contract would not be renewed.

I was glad in a way. I knew that I would never again try to coach basketball.

A few days prior to this visit, I had received a letter from the school board regarding the principalship of the Homewood Heights school at Creve Coeur. I had been highly recommended to them, and all I had to do was sign the contract and return it to them. I could visit with them at my convenience and the salary was considerably more than what I was getting.

I didn't sign it and send it—I *took* it.

There were two schools here. One building at the top of the hill, and the other at the bottom. There was a little apartment built in a garage at a home near the school. It was very neat and pretty and Joy liked it fine.

The day we moved, we arrived at the house about ten, and were busy unloading when a lady from a house across the street came over and told us not to leave when we were done unloading, as she had lunch all fixed for us.

This was typical behavior from all the neighbors in this little community, and in just a few days, we had settled into a routine. I devoted some time to planning for the fall term and also took a job with the Peoria Creamery, who had advertised for someone with a knowledge of chemistry for a summer position.

My job was to test each churn of butter for moisture and salt before it was boxed for sale. This didn't take long, and since the boss kept everybody busy doing something, I was liable to be assigned to brushing lids to the big wood tubs or scraping the large heads of cheese that would later be cut into smaller portions for sale to the stores. I didn't really mind any of these assignments. The work had to be done, and the seasonal helpers were the logical ones to do it. The regular help, some who had been with the company for years, had their own special responsibilities.

One job that I dreaded was defrosting the pipe coils in the cold room, where the temperature was kept below freezing (actually, at or near zero degrees Fahrenheit). We would put on extra coveralls, sweaters, gloves, and anything else that we could find to keep warm. At noon, we would leave the extra clothes on when we went to the nearby restaurant. The people who worked there were accustomed to this unusual July and August dress and didn't pay too much attention to us; strangers looked at us like we were crazy. Some of them were wearing very little.

Eventually, I was asked to assist Homer, our foreman and ice-cream maker. Now, this was really what I was cut out for!

We made vanilla, strawberry, chocolate, black walnut, and of course, special orders. We purchased the mix, which came to us in metal cans. This mix was poured into the freezer, the flavoring and extras, like nuts or cherries, were added to the mix, and it was frozen until it was just right to be run out into boxes or other containers, then put into the cold room to continue freezing.

Of course, there was usually a little left over, not enough to fill a container, but too much to leave in the freezer for the next batch. I loved that part of the drainings that ended up in a Dixie cup (pint size) for me to sample. Of course, I had to check each freezer to be sure that it was good enough to sell. It was not long until the company went out of business. I guess I hit the ice cream a little too hard.

There was one other thing that contributed to our summer. Joy saw an ad in the paper about a canoe for sale. It was an Old Town sailing canoe, eighteen feet long, complete with sail and leeboards. Thirty dollars. Just like the one that I had paddled with Mrs. Waterman in 1936, it was exactly the kind that I had always wanted, but never thought that I would have.

We jumped in the car and in less than an hour, it was resting quietly on our lawn. I hoped that it would float; it did: Like a yellow leaf in autumn; like a yellow water lilly. It was a little heavier than Hiawatha's.

This was a very good summer for the Jacksons. Joy had gotten a part-time job at the Hiram Walker's Brewery, I had my job at the Creamery Company, and we had a neighborhood of nice people who cheerfully waved when they passed. It was too good to be true.

I, of course, was registered for the draft (Pearl Harbor didn't exactly go unnoticed). I was not too surprised to find that I was 1-A. The famous "Greetings" letter informed me that I could expect to be called sometime this fall, but not later than November. I do not have the letter, and I don't recall the exact wording, but I don't need to. I knew then and I know now what they meant. Some of my friends and neighbors were in the same boat, including at least one board member.

My first thought was that I would have time to get the school started. That didn't last long, though, because I had a school board that had been good to me. I had neighbors with children and I was responsible, in a way, for the general welfare of them and the children. It would be better if we could get a new principal before school started so that there would not be a disruption in the school term.

I immediately contacted the board members and told them of my problem. If they could not find a teacher, I would stay as long as I could, otherwise I would let the new teacher begin the term on the regular date.

There was one thing that I had not considered. I was under contract to the board and the school. I was drafted while under that contract. Therefore, when I was discharged from the service, I would have employment under the terms of that contract. I was to notify them as soon as I was discharged, and there would be a place on the faculty. What wonderful people.

Fortunately, someone knew of a teacher who might like to have the job. They hired the teacher, but I never met him (or her).

Joy and I made a trip to visit our folks and inform them of the interruption in the professional life of what I thought might be a great teacher, and to arrange for a place for her to live closer to our parents. This got to be a little more important now that Joy was pregnant, expecting a new little Jackson in May.

My grandfather was dead and Grandmother was having a difficult time living alone during the winter in their house on Eighth Street in Lincoln.

Also, Joy was having a problem. She had a fibroid tumor in her uterus which had the doctor worried. He wanted to monitor the growth for a while before deciding not what was best, but what was possible.

Under the circumstances, being close to our physician and the hospital was of paramount importance, and Joy agreed to the arrangement.

We stored some of the things we owned, and moved to Lincoln.

A house with two dominant women is a trying place to live at its very best. When both women are trying to get along, it becomes bearable. At least, most of the time. Both Joy and Grandma put up a pretty good front when I was around, but I could sense the strain between the two.

We had been in Lincoln only a few days when I got a call from the grade school superintendent, Mr. Harry F. Augspurger. The young man who was teaching "shop" in the junior high school had accepted another position, and had told the superintendent that I was in town and was unemployed, seeking temporary work while waiting to be called into the armed forces.

Mr. Augspurger had been my algebra teacher in high school, had been involved in boy-scouting and church work with me, so he knew me pretty well. He told me that he was pretty sure that he could get a deferment for me that would extend my call to the service from November until March, and would give me four months of teaching time. It was a deal, and a most fortunate one for me, as I had plenty of things to worry about without having to leave Joy alone at this particular time.

Time came for another visit with the doctor about Joy's pregnancy, and this time, the verdict was nothing short of heart-breaking. The doctor laid a hand on each of our shoulders, and, looking straight at me, said, "Harry, I can save your wife or I can save the baby. I cannot save them both."

Joy, just as directly, looked at the doctor, and said, "He doesn't have anything to say about it, we will save the baby."

Preparing for the Service

Apparently, the tumor was larger than he expected it to get. Joy's physical condition was not the best, and the doctor did not think that Joy could survive both the birth and the tumor surgery at the same time. As far as she was concerned, the case was closed. Nothing more was said about it. Fortunately, her time was near, which shortened the period of expectancy. She gave her true feelings away one day, when she said to me as I was getting out of bed after one of my not-so-deep sleeps, "Harry, I am not bringing our baby back to this house. Go to Hallsville and see if you can find us a place to live. It is going to be all right."

I found the house, rented it, and hoped for the best. Having another place to live gave both of us a brighter outlook on life, and about six o'clock P.M. on the eighteenth of May, 1943, Kenneth Keith Jackson was born. His mother survived. He was six pounds, fourteen ounces and sound as a dollar. Joy said only, "I told you so," and went to sleep smiling. She didn't even hear me say, "Thank you; I love you."

Several weeks later, the tumor was removed and Joy had a chance to regain her strength.

We settled into the new home, which was "new" only to us, and enjoyed our life in the little town of Hallsville. We knew everyone in town and made many friends in the short time we were there.

Teaching in the Junior High in Lincoln was a pleasant experience for me. I thoroughly enjoyed the children and was accepted readily by the other faculty members. One drawback was having to commute seventeen miles to work. There were evening activities in Lincoln that I must attend, and commuting was both tiring and expensive. I was tired of moving so often, but we decided to look for a house in Lincoln after Christmas.

Kenneth Cecil, my nephew and Kenneth Keith's godfather, would be home on leave over the holidays, and for the first time, get to see his namesake. He lost no time getting to our house to help trim little Ken's first Christmas tree. It also was the last Christmas that we all would share. I think that we all felt that it would be, but no one mentioned it.

After Christmas, we moved into a nice little house owned by Claude Workman. Claude was the man who thought that we boys on the threshing run were not hauling our share of bundles. He was willing to rent the house, but let it be known that we were expected to take care of it, and that we would be responsible for any damage that we did to it. I was a little amused at that, as I was not in the habit of ruining the landlord's property, usually leaving it in better condition than when I rented it.

We got along just fine. We paid our rent on time. He made regular walks down our street to ascertain that his house was still there. I understood how he felt. I didn't know at that time whether I would ever own a house or not. It wasn't likely, but I reserved judgment.

My brother-in-law, Carl Boatman, and I were to report for duty on the fourteenth of March. That gave me less than a week to make final arrangements, most of which, I thought, had been made. We had comfortable quarters for Joy and Kenny. They were near places to shop and our parents.

The house rent was due, so, one evening we took our money to the landlord. I was about to hand him the envelope when I casually mentioned that I would not be seeing them for a while, since I had been called for duty by the draft board. I also told him that he didn't need to worry about paying the rent, I would have enough money, but in case of an emergency, my father or my brother would pay him.

There was a sudden dead silence. Then, he said, "No. Pay in the service is not reliable, and we will have to have the house a month from now."

We were paid up until Tuesday, so I put our rent money back in my pocket, and said, "All right, you can have your house Monday evening. Good night." There was no "Good luck," or any other acknowledgment forthcoming as we left them.

When we got "home," Joy picked up the newspaper and started to read the ads. Suddenly, she found one that caught her attention. It was a house for sale, five hundred dollars down and twenty dollars a month. We were to see Henry Bertsche.

I knew Mr. Bertsche well. He operated a tire and battery service store, was a good man, and Joy and I went to see him the next morning. The house was empty. We could go see it, and if we wanted it under the terms that he had advertised we could move in immediately.

We had a little money, but Joy would need it to live on until my first navy payday and her allotment check arrived. What could we sell? A boat (not our Old Town canoe) some other odds and ends, and finally, the car. Joy had been out most of the day while I did some cleaning in the house where we were living. About three o'clock, she walked in the front door and handed me five one-hundred dollar bills. By five o'clock, the house was ours.

Everybody that was available was "turned to" for cleaning detail, and Monday night we slept in our own house. I have never rented a house since, and have never lived in one that was as truly a "home" as that one.

As ordered, my brother-in-law, Carl Boatman and I were at the railroad station in Clinton ready to board the Illinois Central's finest troop train bound for Chicago for the final "sorting" of the fit versus the unfit. Or so it seemed to us.

Upon arrival at the designated place, we were given a choice: Army, Navy or Marines? Carl and I both selected Navy and were shown where to go. Finally, a final medical exam for which we were stripped of all clothing which was put into a bag to be mailed home. "Keep your watch and wedding ring." A few minutes later, I glanced back down the line looking for Carl. No Carl. That last medical check had got him. I would have felt lonely, if it hadn't been for the three or four hundred men in the same room with me.

Sea bag, ditty bag, hammock, blankets, clothing, shoes. I don't know how they did it, but all of the clothing fit. During my tour of duty, I wore it with pride.

I don't know where the guides took the army and marine recruits, but the navy men formed a very ragged line and were marched to a very large building, which was to be our home for whatever time we would be considered boots. All the way over, heads and shoulders were visible through the windows of other dormitory buildings, and calls of "You'll be sorry!" were only telling us what we already knew!

We were in charge of a "pusher" whose job was to tell us forty or fifty times each day, "This ain't no boy scout troop!" Then, there were the usual round of immunization shots, the trip to the dentist, and the typical navy nomenclature by which the bathroom (toilet) became the head, your bed was the sack, the floor was the "deck" and a place to go for meals was the mess. Believe me, the mess was, next to the sack, the best times of the day.

There were regular times set aside for drill. For that, we were taken out on the big black-top area known as the grinder. We did not look forward to those times. March in the Chicago area can be an ugly, cold, windy and just all-around miserable experience, even without the colds that we all seemed to have and the fever and muscleache from the shots.

We were taken to the swimming pool to try to pass the swimming requirement which was to swim the length of the pool. About half of the hundred and sixty-man company made it. We were all "passed" anyway. One man had to be pulled out of the water before he drowned.

The physical fitness test consisted of "chinning" yourself on a horizontal bar suspended about six feet above the floor. Six times was a passing grade. About ten of us passed that one. I couldn't believe it. Any of the men that I grew up with on the farm could have chinned themselves ten times easily, and some could have done it with one arm. In the old country school days, we used a tree limb for the bar. But this was wartime, and the physical development would have to come later.

These activities were "musts." If there was time left over after the musts, it was usually spent on the grinder.

There was one piece of advice that has been handed down in the armed forces: *don't volunteer for anything!* That is good advice ... normally. Sometimes you have a little piece of information, or a gut feeling that alters the situation: Our pusher went on leave, and left us on our own resources for nearly a day. Thank God. The man who replaced him was a real gentleman, quiet and easy-going, but thorough and reasonable. One day, he came and stood near me, talking to some of the men. When they moved away, he whispered to me, "There will be a man coming in soon, asking if anyone can type. Tell him yes!"

The result was that I sat behind a desk out in the hall, from eight P.M. until midnight. Every hour, I typed on the appropriate form the hour and that all was "all" secure. The rest of the time, I read or called home or visited with staff that came by. I never stepped on the grinder the rest of the tour of duty in boot camp.

There was one big day coming up. We each met with an officer to determine where we might fit the best or where we were needed the most.

My man was a Lieutenant Commander and seemed to be a most pleasant man to talk to. He had a stack of papers that apparently had some information about me.

"I see that you are a teacher."

"Yes, sir."

"Have training in chemistry and some of the other sciences."

"Yes, sir. Some."

"Passed the test for work as a radioman."

"I didn't know that I had passed it, Sir." (Actually, I didn't see how I could possibly have passed it as I had guessed at most of the answers).

"What are your choices for assignment?"

I had not given any serious consideration to what kind of work I would like to do, and in fact, I didn't think it would make much difference. To avoid appearing too stupid, I suddenly barked out, "Signal Corps or radio, or supply." That was all I could think of quickly enough to answer.

"That's not where we need you. Where we need you the most is in the hospital corps. How about hospital apprentices?"

I told him I didn't like hospitals.

"How about Hospital Corpsman?" I had come up one pay grade.

"I don't think I would be good at hospital work."

"Look, Son, I'm busy. You are, as of right now, a Pharmacist Mate Third Class! Get out of here."

I got. I had gone from seventy-eight dollars a month to one hundred twenty. Don't worry. I earned it.

My boot days were about over. I got a call to report to a ward (I forget the number) at Great Lakes Naval Hospital for duty. Limited duty. In other words, just until they made up their minds where else to put me.

I reported to the ward, was told that they were shorthanded and I might be asked to work in various places. First, I report to classes every morning. Classes usually were given by a nurse on such topics as surgical procedures, care of the dead and dying, battle fatigue, use of the bed pan, proper dressing of wounds, and the list went on. We had about one half to one hour of exposure to each of these. The rest of the day was spent in the ward doing odd jobs. These are jobs that must not be taken lightly. We didn't have little candy striper girls running around to do them, and the work had to be done.

I got in one morning in surgery. That was plenty. A young man had walked into a fighter plane propeller, and they were rebuilding his face from his high-school graduation picture.

The next week, I got to go home on boot leave. I got home on the 7:26 train, and it wasn't very long until I had a paint brush in my hand. Joy had worked wonders fixing up our house, and I could see that she and Kenny would be comfortable while I was gone. I got to see all of my family while I was home but spent most of my time working on the house which had been neglected for so long.

I thoroughly enjoyed my leave, but like all leaves, it had to come to an end. I left home on the evening train for Chicago. We did not have a car, so Joy planned to walk with me to the station, leaving little Kenny with her sister, Elizabeth.

Kenny had been so good all of the time that I was home, even up to suppertime, but the little rascal knew beyond a doubt that Dad was going to leave him, and he cried so loud I think they could have heard him in Chicago. There was no reasoning with him, and I had to leave with him crying his heart out. Joy finally had to leave me and go back to him. That was the worst hour that I spent in my service career.

At Great Lakes, I went directly to O.G.U. (outgoing unit) for assignment to duty. We all sat around in a big room waiting for our name and assignment to be posted on the bulletin board. After a couple of hours, there it came. To U.S. Naval Hospital, St. Albans, Long Island, New York. For duty. That implied that I was not going to a school someplace to learn what a third class pharmacist mate is expected to do.

There was considerable scuttlebutt around the bulletin board, but the gist of it was that St. Albans Naval Hospital was as good as any place and better than most. I hoped so. I could at least enjoy the free train ride. After a hurried phone call to Joy, I packed my gear, did most of what we were told to do, and the next day, was given nice quarters in the corpsmen's barracks on the hospital grounds. I had arrived.

I was a country boy who had grown up to be a country man. My experience in a big city consisted of a few trips to Chicago and St. Louis, never staying long enough to get the feel of the place. New York City, with the neighboring ocean, rivers and mountains, had been always been a storybook dream, and here I am, ready to take the bait.

We reported to the Chief Petty Officer, who seemed to be in charge. He welcomed us and told us how to find our bunks. Three of us, or maybe more, went to the second floor to a big room, open in the center, but lined with cubicles around the wall. Each cubicle had four bunks. Two on each side, one above the other with two lockers, side by side, on the open side of the cubicle.

We made our beds, establishing possession. The dorm was not nearly full, so we all got lower bunks. We did not have to report for duty until the next morning, and had liberty until then. Liberty was no problem. We knew how to handle that, so we were off to see the sights, and as you may have guessed, the first thing that we wanted to see was Times Square!

My companions were Dick Travin, a salesman from Chicago, and Frank Keech, an attorney-at-law from Glens Falls in upstate New York. This little trip of exploration was only one of many that the three of us enjoyed together, although I shared liberty time with many wonderful companions over the next two years. I never dreamed that I would serve my total service time on the same base, and that it would be in a place like St. Albans. It didn't take me long to find out that there was plenty of work to be done. This hospital was a busy place and very shortly was going to be even busier. Every one of us was badly needed.

The next morning, we reported to the officer-of-the-day, whom informed us of our assignment to duty. All were assigned before we left Great Lakes, or so I was told. All names were called and told where to go. I was the last one called. No place for me to go, there was no indication at all that anyone wanted me!

Finally, he said, "Go to the Master-of-Arms Chief. He can use you."

He could use me, all right, and I spent the first two weeks patrolling the main hallway, just looking after things, not to take care of anything that happened, but to keep it from happening in the first place.

There was also a note of warning: "Stay out of the wards." It seems that some of the MAs had been inclined to spend more time visiting with the night nurses than they did patrolling the corridors. After a few lonely nights walking a half mile each way, with only an occasional patient coming in from liberty, you were ready to talk to anyone, and the nurses and corps WAVES were the best the navy could provide.

I was wondering about a change of duty. Once you were assigned, you could not apply for change of duty for thirty days. So, I waited. While I waited, I walked the corridors with less and less enthusiasm. One thing bugged me. Periodically, hanging on the wall, I would see a sign that said, SEE YOUR EDUCATIONAL SERVICES OFFICER!

Well, I figured he didn't mean right now, at midnight. So the next afternoon, I did just that. He was Lieutenant (junior grade) Charles Bernhard. Right then and there, a deep friendship was born.

I walked through the open door, saw Lieutenant Bernhard at a desk. There was a WAVE officer sitting with her back to me, so I couldn't tell much about her, but Lieutenant Bernhard introduced her. Her name was G. Alison Raymond and I later learned that she was a sharp, no-nonsense lady.

After the introduction, Lieutenant Bernhard asked, "What can I do for you?" I told him about seeing the signs in the corridor and that I didn't see much future in being a Master-at-Arms. Did he have any suggestions?

He explained about the work of the Educational Services and then asked about me. He nodded his head when I said that I was a teacher, and asked about what experience I had. I told him, then he said, "How would you like to work for me?" He explained about their service to the patients and staff, and I said I would like it, and would come as soon as my thirty days were up, which would be in a little less than two weeks.

He said, "Take your duty tonight, and come in tomorrow afternoon. I will see that it is approved by Personnel." I was a member of the Educational Service Staff for the rest of my tour of duty, and for the last six months or so, (I didn't know about it until some time later) I was frozen to the base, ineligible for transfer or even for any extended leave.

I enjoyed the work. We had carts on which we carried books and other supplies to the wards so that non-ambulatory patients could take courses and receive credit toward a diploma at whatever level he desired, even the higher disciplines of mathematics and literature. Ambulatory patients could work as a group, and they enjoyed that—especially when the course was being taught by one of the WAVES, and I didn't blame them for that.

I enjoyed meeting the men and talking with them, trying to ascertain what I could do for them that would benefit them the most.

One day, I got a message from the office, I was to report to a commander (whose name I have forgotten) right away, like now! I reported, all right, scared to death about what might have happened, although most emergency messages came from the officer of the day.

A marine outside the door checked to see if I was really me, (name and serial number) and ushered me into the inner sanctum.

He informed me that the Red Cross had a whole room full of radios that wouldn't play. "Son, you are going to start a radio repair class."

"Sir, I don't know a thing about radio."

"Well, you soon will."

Then, he explained what I was going to do: first, find a room to serve as a shop. Find a patient, ambulatory, who was a radioman, preferably first class, who could teach other men how to make the necessary repairs to get those damned radios to working and get those gray ladies (Red Cross volunteers) off his back. Give the radioman liberty three nights out of four.

"How about tools?" As of then I had open gang plank. That is, I could go and come from the base any time I wanted to. I was to go to any company or store that carried tools and beg, borrow, or steal what we needed to get the job done.

I went directly to the office. As I entered, he just said, "How did you make out?" The rascal had set me up for it himself and this was only a small part of what he had in mind for Educational Services.

Over the next year, his plan grew into a 60' × 90' shop in the basement of the hospital. There were classes and projects designed to fit a given problem, but in general, if a patient, because of physical injury, could not go back to his old job, it was our plan to help him learn skills that would enable him to work at another. Someone somewhere had seen in my record that I had been a shop teacher. That it had been only a junior high school was not a big factor.

We had instructors gleaned from the patient population, and rewarded with more frequent liberty. For more extensive work in some areas, such as photography, Red Cross Gray Ladies were superb. What we had was a very good technical high school.

For me, the greatest satisfaction came with a post-op patient who needed to use certain muscles as much as possible to strengthen them. Or, in one or two cases, patients who were in need of psychological observation or treatment. If a surgeon came to see me (or more likely called me to see him), he would explain what he wanted the patient to do. For example, strengthen an arm and shoulder muscle group. What did I suggest? Using a plane to shape pieces of wood to make something to send home to his mother or girl. At least, that was the general idea.

The word got around, and we gradually built up a very busy little community of our own, in some cases, valuable because it gave the patient someplace to go other than their ward. We tried especially to put these patients to work at something.

Twice a year, the hospital was visited by an Admiral. I guess, it was a regular inspection type of visit. Imagine how a third-class Pharmacist Mate felt when an Admiral walked into the shop. I am not sure now who his escort was, but I think that it was Captain Sprague, at that time, the Chief of Surgery. They looked around, spoke briefly to a couple of the gray ladies in the photo lab, then headed for me.

Captain Sprague introduced me to the Admiral *(My God, the Captain knew my name!)* who asked me some questions, how did I know which muscles to treat? I said I had a mean old biology teacher one time who made me learn them. He laughed, and said if it suits the Captain, it suited him. Good-bye.

A few weeks later, the word came, saying that the responsibility was too great for an enlisted man, and they put an officer in charge of the shop.

Bernhard told me I would be relieved, but that I had been recommended for a commission, and that he and the Admiral had approved. I had mixed feelings about that, but I doubted if it would go through. It didn't. It got as far as the Bureau of Medicine and Surgery. They would not release me.

In a couple of days, a lieutenant showed up. He was a patient, but was being discharged from the hospital and had not as yet been reassigned.

He walked in, said, "I'm Lieutenant so and so (I forget his name) and I'm in charge here. Get your things out of the office, I'll take all phone calls."

Since it was early in the morning, there were probably fifteen or more men just standing around visiting. I always had a pot of coffee in the little office, and all the men knew that they were welcome to lounge in or around the office and to have coffee there.

To a man, they rinsed the cups, put them on the little shelf, and walked out, back to their wards. There they stayed.

I had to figure this out. Any sailor that has been on a base for over a year, if he is any good at all, will have a few friends in high places. I had. All I had to do was figure out how to use them. So, I waited.

The first order came, "Jackson, this shop is a mess, sweep it up, and empty the trash before the trash collectors come."

I walked around checking the waste baskets. They were all empty and clean. The hospital custodians did all of that every night. I told him, "If it isn't satisfactory, call maintenance."

A few men who had not been present earlier came in and started work on their projects. "What are they messing around in here for?" says his honor, the Lieutenant. I told him. He only grunted.

This went on for two or three more days. No sign of Bernhard. I couldn't call the office because what's-his-name had the phone covered. I stopped by the office on the way to chow and found out that Bernhard was in Washington, D.C., but would be back the next day.

He was, but was very busy and it was afternoon before he got my report.

In the meantime, business was pretty black in what used to be "my" shop. About mid-morning, the phone rang. The Lieutenant answered.

Now, it just happened that one day, in a flash of foresight, I had asked the phone men if I could have a phone in the photo lab. If you were developing film, there is no way you can run out into the office to take a call. Actually, I never knew of such a need, but it sounded good and the men ran the line, installed the phone, and gave me contact with the outside world.

When the phone rang that morning, I nonchalantly walked into the photo lab and listened in. The conversation went something like this:

"Shop. Lieutenant So-and-So speaking."

"May I speak to Jackson, please?"

"I am the manager here, now. No one else uses the phone."

"I am sorry, but this is surgery, and I want to speak to Jackson."

"I will be glad to take the message.'

All of the above calls from surgery were a feminine voice. I knew the nurse well as she had sometimes brought word to me from the doctor, and she was not about to put up with this gaff. She didn't have to. A very masculine voice appeared on the surgery phone.

"This is Captain Sprague talking. Now, just what in the hell is going on down there? I want to talk to Jackson and I want to talk to him, now!"

I headed for the office as if I didn't know what had been going on, walked into the office, and took the phone from the "manager."

"It is a long story, Sir, but in short, my main job now is janitor."

"I don't have time to listen now but . . . " he went on to state a question about a patient.

I said, "I don't know, Sir. Most of the men have quit coming and I haven't seen (the patient)."

It was a cold day in that shop. The next morning, the Lieutenant didn't show. He didn't the next morning, either. I couldn't resume my old job, as I was ordered not to. So I called the Educational Services Office and asked Lieutenant Bernhard, "Where is Lieutenant So-and-So?"

"Well, Harry, the good Lieutenant is on his way to San Diego. I hope he was a good trip."

I couldn't help saying, "I don't." That was the first and only time that a Navy officer called me by my first name.

From then on, the shop stayed as if it had been betrayed. It never did, as long as I was there, get its full quota of patients. The other programs grew larger and stronger.

It was not long after this that my discharge points had added up and I went home to stay.

However, there are a few nonrelated incidents that I want to mention. I didn't spend all of my time in the Educational Services, or in the "shop."

When I arrived at St. Albans I could see that life in a Naval Hospital might take a little getting used to. The main corridor was over a mile long, there were two large mess halls, and I don't know how many wards there were. I was told that the hospital was built to accommodate five thousand patients and that there were over two thousand doctors, nurses, and hospital corps. I could believe it, because soon after D-Day, scuttlebutt had it that there were seven thousand patients there.

I had liberty three nights, then, on the fourth night, I had the duty. This meant that instead of quitting work at the usual time, I stayed on the job until 9:00 P.M. Then, I could go to the barracks and hope to stay there. Sometimes I could, but I stood a good chance of being called for a special watch, which meant another four hours of doing whatever needed to be done. Usually, extra patient care, because we now had many battle casualties . . . some that were brought to us with the battlefield dressing still on, and needed attention right now. I assume that most of those had been brought in by air-evac, because ambulances could be seen coming in any hour of the day or night.

Some of these were taken directly to surgery, and of course, needed attention in the ward immediately following.

One night, I was assigned to a patient for post-op care, and we had to put him on the top bunk of a three-level bed. I had to have a ladder to take his blood pressure.

Only one time did I have two special watches the same night. I had finished one watch and gone back to the barracks, only to be called out again. This one was a young man in one of the rooms set aside for violent behavior. Fortunately for me, he was asleep.

I read the doctor's instructions, and was relieved to see the last line, "If patient becomes restless, administer one-eighth of morphine." The tools were all laid out nice and handy!

There was no reading material, no radio, and no visitors. I had been on the job for thirteen hours and was tired and sleepy. Also, I had to sit there and watch this patient sleeping like a baby.

I had been there about two hours when the patient moved. Good! Getting restless! I waited awhile, he moved again, and I carried out the doctor's orders. Case closed? Not quite.

I leaned my chair back against the wall to be a little bit more comfortable. I woke up when the day crew came in. I could hear them outside my padded cell. That was when I awakened enough to see that I had a blanket thrown over my shoulders, courtesy of the night nurse. I never found out who it was. Each of them got a box of chocolates in the mail anonymously. That was the only time that I slept on watch.

One night in the late fall, I left the hospital, glad to get away from the monotony of the Master-at-Arms duty that finally ended at 2100 hours. It was a short walk to the barracks building, but the rain was coming down in sheets. Normally, I would have just gone back to the Educational Services office and either waited it out or just gone to sleep. But from the section of the main corridor where I was, it was closer to the barracks than it was to the office, so I headed home.

I got pretty damp, but went on up the stairs to bed. Several of the mates had just came in from their watch and were sitting around visiting. I joined them for a while, and was about to go to bed when a Chief Petty Officer came in and informed us that one of our men was laying on the sidewalk and couldn't make it inside. "You had better go get him," he said.

We all knew the kid, but he was being shipped out within a day or two, and we suggested that he had been on liberty getting good and drunk. Unfortunately, some of the younger sailors thought that was the thing to do, the "last night ashore" bit.

None of us wanted to get wet, but finally, two of us made the break, dragging him between us until we got him inside, up the stairs and to his cubicle. We worked with him until we thought he was capable of undressing and getting to the shower.

We could hear the shower running, but suddenly, someone said he thought he ought to be clean enough by now. Frank Keech, Dick Travin and I looked at each other, and as one, headed for the shower room.

There stood the kid, hat, clothes, shoes and all, standing in the shower of steaming hot water. His face was as red as a beet, and he was grinning from ear to ear. I reached for the faucet to turn the hot water off, but missed it and threw the control clear over, onto the cold.

It worked. He came out, undressed and laid on his sack, with a violent chill. None of us were willing to let him use one of our blankets in the shape he was in, but we finally found something more to cover him.

The next morning, he looked like a ghost, but when we came back to our bunks the next afternoon, he was gone and we never saw him again. *E pluribus Unum.* In God, we trust, but there are times when it is nice to have one or more shipmates handy.

After my more stable assignment to Educational Services, I began exploring the possibility of having Joy and Kenny come to Saint Albans. There were rooms and small apartments available, and several of my friends had their wives renting quarters near the hospital.

Joy was receptive to the idea, and in a few days, I met her at Grand Central Station and introduced her to what was now my hometown, at least for a while. Kenny remembered me, Joy could never have let him forget, and we hit it off really well, especially if there was a train involved.

Occasionally, we would leave Kenny with another couple in the same house and take in a movie. When we just went sightseeing, Kenny went along. We found out that children were not welcome at the theaters, and in some restaurants, but we were never turned away, nor did Kenny ever cause any problem. I just as well say it here as any other place in the narrative, Kenneth Keith didn't, like Topsy, "just grow." He was *raised!*

There were many things in New York City to visit and enjoy, but it was not long until Kenny zeroed in on the zoo. If asked what he wanted to do on some Saturday or Sunday, he would always choose the zoo. His choice alternated between Central Park and the Bronx. He had favorites in each place, and before I left Saint Albans, he could name every animal in the guide book. I was so proud of my wife and child!

I was surprised, one day, to see a figure coming toward me that could only be one person: my nephew, Kenneth Cecil. I had received one or two letters from him, but never dreamed that he would be ashore where we could meet.

I took the rest of the day off as far as any work was concerned, then took him home with me to see Joy and Kenny.

He was starved for fresh fruit, and when we passed our neighborhood grocery, he spied some choice cuts of watermelon. I knew we were going to have all he wanted, and told the grocer that he wanted a whole watermelon. He told me he sold it only by the piece, and I told him we would pay the by-the-piece price. He said he couldn't do that. Then, I said, "Cut it into pieces and we will buy all of them."

He just shook his head, "No."

By this time, Ken was beginning to get angry. He had just got back from Murmansk, and he was not accustomed to dealing gently with little problems like this. He gently moved closer to the storekeeper, and said, "Mister, we are going to buy that watermelon and pay you for it. If you do not agree, I will step to that door, and in ten minutes, this store will be a shambles. How much?"

The sidewalk was crowded with sailors just coming out on liberty. Most of them were ambulatory patients, many were fleet marines wounded in the South Pacific landings, and they certainly were not sissies. We got the melon and enjoyed a wonderful reunion with the boy that grew up in the same house with me.

On the eighth day of May 1945, I had barely had time to get the shop open when I had a call from the officer of the day. Somehow, I knew before I answered the phone that it was some kind of bad news from home. Since Joy and Kenny were with me, it couldn't be one of them. The most logical parent was my mother, who had not been well for years, but tried not to show indications. I could tell it was difficult for the O.D. to tell me, but that is what the message was. My first thought was, "At least, she got to know that it was VE day."

The O.D. said that my papers would be ready for me to pick up as I left the hospital. After a quick call to Joy, I turned the shop over to one of the patients that I knew could handle it, went past the Officer-of-the-Day's office, picked up my leave papers, and left. I did not look at the papers, but how I wished that I had!

It was a mad scramble for Joy to get ready to go home, but finally, we made it to the bus to Jamaica, then by subway to within a short distance from Grand Central. Joy was carrying Kenny, and I was carrying a suitcase in each hand and the ties from my ditty bag around my shoulder. We were rubbing our train time pretty close, and didn't dare stop or slow down as we had to cross a busy street. An elderly man nearby sensed our predicament. He ran up to Joy, took Kenny from her and said, "Follow me!"

We made it. I heard Joy thank the man, but by the time I turned to see him, he was gone. I learned to like New Yorkers soon, and over the months, saw many similar examples of their concern for strangers to their city.

The funeral was held up until Joy and I arrived. Mom's last words were, "Now my boys can come home."

There was one very difficult problem for me to solve. On the train, a Shore Patrol asked to see my papers. I gave them to him and bleached out white as he said, "Son, you can't make it to Lincoln and back in four days!"

It should have been fourteen! The officer of the day saw that I was frozen to the base and was not eligible for leave. What he didn't know was that it did not apply to leave granted in case of death in the family. Or, so I had been told.

The Shore Patrol suggested that when I reached Lincoln, I should contact the Red Cross and try to get an extension. I did that, but the extension was not granted.

I was AOL (absent over leave) and in a deep trouble. It was difficult to anticipate what would happen, so we took it just day by day. I left home the day after the funeral, but left Joy and Kenny in Lincoln for a longer visit with our families.

When I got back to St. Albans, I got a room at a hotel (a cheap one) and called one of the nurses that I knew real well and asked her who the officer of the day would be.

The O.D. was a man I knew well. I had lucked out. Maybe. Sure enough, when I got to the hospital the next morning, my papers had been rewritten with those days as expected day to return. I had a clean slate, thanks to having friends in high places. I called Joy immediately.

Schedules returned to some semblance of normalcy, but V-E day had begun a new era, not only in the hospital, but in the whole country. I had missed the celebration at Times Square, but I didn't mind. I was too interested in what was happening on the Pacific front. And, happen it did! Things happened that only a few people in the world could comprehend at that time, and for many years to come.

Eventually, there was another great day, and it was called V. J. Day. This celebration in the street at Times Square was one of the great days of my Navy career.

I did not make any big wave with the contribution that I made for my country, but the ripple that I did make was done proudly and unselfishly, and it was with mixed feelings that on 17 January, 1946, I said my good-bye around the many familiar sites around the hospital, finally having to stop because the pain of leaving was too great.

I met a young man who was doing the same thing, so we paired up to leave the hospital. We could have remained aboard; our train didn't leave until the next morning, but there is always that feeling that someone might change their mind and prevent our leaving, so we went to a hotel near Grand Central for the night.

The young man's name was Paul Pechinino (Peck for short) and we knew each other well. Our room was comfortable and we decided that we would not "celebrate" in true navy style, but would eat in the hotel dining room and "sack in" early. Peck was going to California; I to Chicago. Sleep is always a rare commodity on the train, we would rest while we could. We visited, and relived experiences until we were amazed to see that it was very late in the evening. We called room service for our late dinner with a bottle of Seagrams Seven for dessert, and called it a night.

The next morning, we were waiting near the boarding area when I looked up and saw several sailors accompanied by a nurse heading our way. It was another well-wishing group of friends and buddies, all patients, that had come to see us off.

We shook hands all around, then the nurse said, "The boys had taken up a little gift so that I could eat well on the way home."

It was a twenty dollar bill pressed into my hand, but I knew that outfit. There wasn't twenty dollars at one time in that bunch. I knew where the money came from, and probably the idea for the trip uptown. Her name was Elizabeth and her main reason for living was so that she could do something nice for someone. "Miss Mac" was one of a kind.

Peck and I went aboard our train and I left it in Chicago. I never saw or heard from Peck again. On Kenny's birthday the following May, I had a long letter from Elizabeth bringing me up-to-date. There were no more; my navy career was completed.

Life after the Navy

When I got off the train in Chicago, the first thing that I noticed was the odor, not strange and repulsive, but familiar and delightful. Suddenly, I realized that I was near the entrance to the Fred Harvey restaurant. Only then did I realize that there *is* a difference. Fred Harvey Company took the first bite out of the "Elizabethan" twenty dollar bill.

I got home on the 7:26 train, possibly the *Ann Rutledge,* and headed across town to Hamilton Street, carrying my Sea Bag, Ditty bag, and that same hammock which had never been used.

Joy didn't have a car, and there was no way for her to meet me. I saw a few minutes later that there were family members gathered there that would have come for me if they had known that was the right train.

I met one person that I knew; the streets were deserted except for him. He looked at me and said, "My God, Jackson, where are you going?" So much for being out of town for two years. I felt badly about being missed!

There was a suitable welcome when I got home a few minutes later from wife, son, and practically my whole family. *They* knew that I had been gone.

The first thing that I did was to get back into civilian clothing. The next thing was to join my family in eating all the good things that Joy and the other girls knew that I liked so well.

My first day home, I had expected to rest and get some idea about what needed to be done to the house. In the Middle West, it is a long time from the middle of January to spring, and you can expect periods of subzero weather any time.

We started by installing a floor furnace, using natural gas in place of coal. A few tubes of window calk was the next consideration, and that was about as far as I got. It was imperative that I contact the school superintendent, as a courtesy first, and secondly, to see if I could start work.

Of course, I could start work. However, there was a bit of a problem. One of the teachers in the Jefferson School District wanted to be relieved and was eagerly waiting for me to get home. Would I consider finishing out the term teaching her third grade? Then, they would get a regular third grade teacher for next fall and I could go back to teaching shop and literature in the Junior High School. I would be on my regular pay rate.

Well, of course, I would do that. I liked to teach lower grades, but had misgivings about my ability. It is a big jump from working with battle-scarred sailors and marines to a room full of third graders (about nine years old).

I didn't just like it; I loved it! It was a new challenge, the children were as cute as can be (even though their main attribute was the ability to talk constantly for six or seven hours out of the day). They were bright, and they had not yet learned many bad habits and ideas from adults.

They liked me okay, too. One favorite little trick was to have their hair ribbon come unfastened so that I would have to re-tie it . . . at least once a day.

One little lad, a very sharp pupil, was in my class again in Junior High. He was in my biology class at University High School in Normal, and in one of my University classes.

I would like to mention names, but I cannot. I never could show favoritism, so I will not name any if I can't name them all.

What a lousy excuse! Of course, I never could name all of my students. They would number in the six-digit category, and I could not remember that many. However, most of them will remember that I said something good to every one of them every day—whether I taught them anything or not.

I renewed my interest in scouting during the winter, and by spring, was beginning to fit in the groove that was expected of me. If you had a talent that could be exploited for the good of the community, you were encouraged to use it, and scouting was still important to me. Of course, I wanted to contribute something to the lives of the boys of scouting age, perhaps because I remembered how badly I wanted to be in the program when I was at that age. I think, now, that I just wanted to be in the program because I liked it! Whatever the reason was, I was in it up to my ears, and continued, in one capacity or another as long as I lived in Lincoln. Ed Dodd was the field executive who one day said, "Jackson, I believe you have had every job in scouting!" I didn't though. I never had been a Cub Scout Den Mother.

After school was out, I began to think about resuming my education. The handwriting was on the wall. If you stay in this profession, you had better have a degree from a reputable university, complete with the courses required for a major in Education and, in addition, a good strong major in a strictly academic field. Of course, for me, that would be in the sciences.

There were other teachers in the school system that were taking additional education, the result being a car pool that left Lincoln early in the morning and didn't return until late afternoon. I wonder how many miles I traveled on old Route 66 with the Martin sisters, Blanche and Marie; Raymond Hitchcock, Lee Stults, Bob Taylor, and from time to time, others as we headed for what was then called Illinois State Normal University, and an eight-week session of "condensed" coursework. I liked it. I had good instructors, and interesting courses. The students were of all ages and disciplines. I would not have been so relaxed if I could have seen down the road a few years! In my academic career, I attended thirteen consecutive summer sessions! I also graduated without really being a member of any "class" and I have to admit, that I would have liked to have been able to say "class of 19xx" instead of just "graduated in 1951."

Frequently, several of the grade school faculty needed the same course. Then, we would investigate the possibility of a professor coming to us to teach the course. This was arranged by the superintendent and the University Extension Office at the University. It was a good arrangement, saving the necessity of several students traveling at night after a busy day of work. The professor had a more flexible routine, and could leave the campus to meet us at an earlier hour.

I took every extension course that we could arrange. Consequently, I amassed a bunch of credits that did not apply toward my degree, but all of them gave me valuable knowledge and insight that I otherwise would have missed. I never took a college course that was not valuable to me at some time in my career. I think there was one or two that showed me what *not* to do.

Route 66, between Lincoln and Bloomington-Normal, was a two-lane road. Eventually, it was widened. Then, it was made four lanes, and ultimately, an interstate. We teachers were sure that we had worn out four roads. Route 66 is mostly memories for me, a site of many endeavors between Chicago and Albuquerque, and between 1921 and its inception, as an interstate.

I thoroughly enjoyed the years that I taught at the junior high school level, woodworking shop in the mornings and "reading" in the afternoon. In the shop, I tried to find projects that developed specific skills. In the literature classes, I emphasied the stories and poems that were most likely to appeal to that age group and that dealt with subjects and events that they would relate to.

One never knows. One student that always seemed pretty indifferent to literature gave me the impression that he was there because he had to be, and was definitely not really fond of writers, especially poets.

It was about thirty years before I heard from him. He was visiting in our little town just a few miles from our farm home. He telephoned and asked if he could see me for a little while. Of course, I was delighted to hear from him and visit with his nice wife and two little girls.

While we were discussing "old times," he told me how much he had enjoyed the literature classes. He picked several pieces and examples, and sat in my living room, reciting from memory for over an hour.

Then, I knew.

I spent several years as scoutmaster of the troop from the Methodist Church in Lincoln. We were an active troop, and constantly on the lookout for suitable activities that could fit into the time slots afforded by the school schedule.

I told the boys about an outing that I had with Russel Dougherty, who was our local field executive. We had canoed Salt Creek from Lincoln to its confluence with the Sangamon River. This makes a beautiful trip at most any time of year, is near home, and not too far to be picked up if you are lucky enough to have a cooperative wife. Fortunately, Russ and I each had wives who were willing to come pick us up if they were taken out to dinner on the way home. All men are not so lucky.

The idea of a troop canoe trip had never occurred to me. There was a major problem with finding enough canoes for a whole troop as well as tents and hauling. It was winter when we first mentioned it, but by spring, I had enough canoes borrowed. I went to the Army Surplus store and bought shelter-halves, and the troop had a pancake supper to raise money for a two-wheel trailer that I had built by Shears Machine Shop. I had to plan and build the canoe rack for it, but when completed, it would haul six canoes on the rack, and all other supplies in the bed.

I still had my beloved Old Town eighteen-footer, but most of the borrowed canoes (and one kyack) leaked. I used roofing tar, glue, moss, paper and anything else I could get to plug holes. Most of them had not been used for a long time, and in later seasons when I took trips for other troops or just boys that wanted to go, I bought canoes and put a stop to the aggravating leaks.

The trip with my troop was a huge success, and the word spread. For several years, I took two or three five-day trips each year, sandwiching them in before the summer session at the university. It fulfilled a need for adventure that the boys needed, and later, I charged a nominal fee for the five-day trip. I had boys that couldn't pay a lump sum pay a little at regular intervals so that by spring, their trip was paid for. Many of the boys went each year, and some of them never outgrew them!

I did do one sneaky trick: when someone paid a deposit on the fee, I put the money in a little sack and put it in my desk drawer, where every pupil in the room knew where it was and I never removed it. There was never one penny stolen. Of course, I never let a large amount accumulate, but no one had a large amount at that time.

Altogether, I took twenty-two trips, over most of the navigable streams in Illinois, and spent over one hundred nights out. When I would be at home over weekends, I had trouble sleeping in a bed. So much for (sometimes cold and muddy) river banks.

We enjoyed talking to fishermen and other people that we met along the rivers, and on those streams we used most frequently, some of the folks watched for us and would come down to water's edge to visit.

On one trip on the Illinois River, north of Peoria, we saw a lovely craft bearing down on us, apparently wondering about us. It was large enough to accommodate all of the boys and we visited for an hour or so, just drifting along drinking cold cokes and visiting. They had a lot of questions about how we organized and planned, how we slept, if I was a good cook, and so on. Finally, the man turned to his wife and said, "I surely wish I could go with them."

Tom Sawyer will never die.

I took my last canoe trip with young people in the middle 1950s with a troop of Mariner Girl Scouts from Holy Trinity Church in Bloomington, and a group from University High School in Normal. These were the only trips I took with girls, whose biggest worry was that they wouldn't do everything as well as the boys did. Bless them all! They did.

Summer of 1949

One day in early summer of 1949, Maurice and Frances drove up and parked in front of the house in a brand new Studebaker Commander, the smaller of the new line of cars so bravely offered by the Studebaker company. We all went over it carefully, trying to decide whether we liked it or not as it was so different from other cars on the market. It was the first car that I could stand beside and look over the top without stretching.

It was then that Maurice informed me that we were going to take a trip right after summer school. There was a three-week break before the school term, and we were heading west!

There was no argument from Joy, Kenny, or me. Kenny was six, a very good age for him to see new country, and it was certainly time for a break for Joy and me. Marcellen was a preteen, and as expected did not say much, but did not miss anything either. Six of us? In that little car? Absolutely. When the time came for us to leave, we packed luggage and people and had plenty of room.

That trip, to this day, ranks very near the top of my totem pole of life's pleasures.

The first part of the trip was a repeat of the route taken in 1940; a stop at Sulfur, Oklahoma, with Aunt Naome and her girls were probably the high point with Frances, as both of my sisters were always fond of them. Millie's husband, Bob Jones, just couldn't seem to do enough for us, capping off sundry courtesies, by taking us to Ada for one night of the annual rodeo, which to us "corn belt farmers" was a rare treat.

Our visit to the old Texas neighborhood was limited to a couple of days, as Clyde and Helen Messenger were planning to go to the mountains of New Mexico and we decided to drive together as far as the Cimarron country. Then we would go on to Carlsbad Cavern and other sites, finally north through Colorado to the Garden of the Gods, Seven Falls, and other scenic areas.

Of course, we enjoyed the scenery, the people, and even the new car, but the real value was manifested in my association with my precious sister and her family. Memories that last a lifetime and do not weaken or diminish with age, but serve only to grow and strengthen the love that we had for each other.

The summer of 1949 was not all fun and games. Joy's parents were in deep trouble, trying to be self-supporting, but her father could not work because of his failing sight, and her mother could not support them with what she could earn doing house work.

I suggested that we rent them a little place and each of their four children pay the rent every fourth month. They could do some gardening to help out. It was quickly pointed out that there were three good reasons why that would not be possible; a brother and two sisters who either would not or could not be responsible for that expense. I knew that they were right; jobs were scarce and wages were low. Contrary to much of the propoganda from political circles, the Depression was not over, and I knew it as well as anyone.

I knew when I suggested my next plan that it was even less practical than the other. It was that we buy a small place, give it to the folks for their lifetime, then sell it and hopefully get our money back. No dice.

My brother-in-law, Carl, had purchased a schoolhouse that was no longer used, two acres of land, and with lots of work and good planning, was gradually producing a lovely home. Across the road and a few roads north was a tract of land that had lots of good grass, a few trees and a gentle slope down to a graveled road on the north end and the intersecting road on the west. It formed one end of a tract on good farmland, but was not tillable for row crops because of the slope. Joy and I recognized it as a good building site, found the owners, and were surprised when we met him and his wife that they would be willing to sell three acres of it. We really wanted the entire plot, but didn't have enough money to buy that much and still start construction on a small house. Later, we did buy the additional plot, making a total of 6.08 acres. We planted nearly an acre with a mixture of Jack Pine and Red Pine, which in a few years became a beautiful grove.

We constructed about half of the house so the folks could move in, and it took us three years before I got the rest of it finished.

Carl helped the folks a lot with work when he could, and the others made many kinds of helpful contributions, in any way they could. Only once was there a hint that it would be nice if I would deed the property to the folks. No deal; the place was theirs as long as they lived, but the deed was mine! At that time, I thought it would make a fine retirement property, and it would have, but the angels smiled on various subjects, as yet unknown to me, who very effectively changed our lives significantly.

There were experiences, both good and not so good, in the years that Joy and I worked so hard on the Hill Farm. Some of them were merely amusing: Dan Boatman was a fine man, as honest as anyone could be, but also a schemer. One of his habits was to relate to me how much Carl did for them; and to Carl, how much I did for them! A classic example of playing both ends against the middle! Carl and I had many a good laugh about it. There was no deceit in Carl Boatman, then or ever. He is a good brother-in-law and a fine gentleman, and we have been friends for many years.

Work on that little place in the country certainly took its toll, not only financially, but in time and good old hard muscle work. Electricity was supplied to that neighborhood by REA, and they were very nice people. The only drawback was that they would not bring in electrical power until there was a building. I didn't have a building. Furthermore, it would be some time before I did have one if I had to cut every board by hand.

I don't know for sure if I recalled the good Reverend Cremeans and his book on *How to Combat Adversity* or not, but I must have, because I sure enough did combat the adversity of building a house with only hand tools. I also took time to remember my great grandfather and my grandfather and how they built the fine house and barn; beautifully fitted joints and everything square and plumb. Then, I went to work, I surely was glad that it was a small house!

It was essential that I use every minute that I had either at my job or out on the hill. Many days, I worked until dark, then by gasoline lantern light until I was too tired to do any more.

Eventually, I had enough done to call it building, and the folks could move into the part that I had relatively weather proof, with electricity.

The next spring, I started on the part that had a basement. Basements have to be dug, either by man or by machine. I didn't have a machine and couldn't afford to hire one (besides, it would have ruined Bethyl's flower bed). So, I dug a hole $12' \times 24' \times 6'$

deep. Two of my teaching buddies, Bob Taylor and Paul Marshal, worked one day and got to a finishing stage, ready to be formed to pour the concrete.

I had hammered away at my education and finally, in the summer of 1951, I was enrolled for the last time in a summer session, ready to graduate in August. Of course, we were still pounding the pavement of Route 66, not having worn it out yet.

One morning (I was driving that week), we were cruising along on the way to classes and contemplating what was in that very dark cloud ahead of us. The concensus was that "somebody is surely getting a hard rain!"

I don't know what caused me to reach down and turn on the radio, but it was just in time to hear the announcer say " . . . damaged the Boatman residence, and was through Atlanta."

"Hey! Hold on! That's my place!"

There was nothing more except the word "tornado." Not one darned thing we could do about it. Some of the riders had final exams scheduled for eight o'clock, and there was no time for further inquiry.

The first thing I did after I parked the car was to head for a telephone, and I thought the best one would be the biology department office (not normally available for student use). The department secretary made the call for Joy in Lincoln, got her on the line, and I told her what I knew. I told her to find out what she could, then call the office so they could get word to me.

In just a few minutes, Joy called back. There was no damage to the buildings. The storm was a quarter of a mile wide, had come to within a few yards of Carl's yard fence, then veered away toward the southeast across a corn field.

We used to compliment Carl on what a strong fence he had built. However, at the first sign of a storm, Carl heads for the basement. So does any other thinking person.

We all passed our exams and I got to attend the commencement exercises, which were held outdoors because of the summer heat. I believe that some of my family attended to see the first university graduate in the family. I had ceased to be impressed.

A New Job

I had barely finished my exams when I had a note delivered to the classroom and handed to me by the professor, Dr. Donald T. Ries, asking me to see Dr. Lamke, head of the biology department in the department office.

Neither of these men were strangers to me. I had at least two courses with each of them, and that is sufficient to learn as much about them as they have learned about you.

Dr. Lamke was not a man to waste much time. He wanted to talk to me about graduate school, and to make sure that I had considered enrolling. We talked about it and he was relieved to know that I had planned to begin fulfilling the course requirements the following summer. It was not likely that graduate level courses would be offered by extension, although some of the education courses might be. They did not require laboratory facilities as the science subject matter did, and the need for science courses at the graduate level was not great. Elementary teachers were notoriously shy about classes in science or mathematics.

Since my curriculum would be designed for a master's degree in science education, there might possibly be a graduate level course in education or psychology offered at some center near enough to attend a night class, saving my summer session time for the science laboratory and field study classes.

As I left his office, Dr. Lamke cautioned me to keep in mind areas in which I might like to do the research leading to the master's dissertation.

I had not given any thought to possibilities for research, except that I did not want to mix science and education. If I did research in science, I would examine the educational aspects of it when the research was completed, or at least terminated.

I had plenty to do without worrying prematurely. I needed to do some work on our house. I was not finished with the final touches to the Hill Farm house, and I did find an extension course, offered in Springfield, that I could attend. My teaching load was normal and was very enjoyable. I thoroughly enjoyed the junior high pupils, and I always considered it a privilege to be their teacher. Discipline problems in the classroom were few and very minor. There were only a few and they had their origin at home or at least, not in school. However, I was not fooled. Any public servant, and especially teachers, will have students who love them, some who dislike them, and a somewhat larger group that just takes you because they have to, to fill up the middle. They are always a challenge and a tremendous responsibility.

I was busy in scouting, but except for the canoe trips or an occasional group activity, I just did the various jobs assigned to commissioners, or other scouters.

I did finally get an extension course at Lincoln. It was a Audio-Visual Education, and dealt with the use of photos, movies, tape recorders and such. It was a relatively new field and I thought it had possibilities. Now, good teachers had used this kind of aid for years, but the course, as taught by Dr. Lincoln Miller, opened avenues of experience that most of us had overlooked.

I reported some of Miller's ideas (and some of mine) to Mr. Augspurger and he put me to work! I became Lincoln's first Director of Audio-Video Education. No increase in salary; just more work. We got what we needed and used what we had. I helped the teachers and did all of the ordering and scheduling of the films. I would have liked to have an occasional John Wayne, but I didn't think that would go over so well.

We all worked hard. That was what we were paid for. The work was pleasant, the faculty was really an extended family, and the pay increases were just barely enough to keep you from hunting a new job. We had a good school board (most of them good friends), but the real steadying influence was Harry F. Augspurger, the city school superintendent and junior high school principal.

I was accustomed to carrying a full load of courses in the summer sessions; but in my haste to finish the requirements I tried for an overload, which required the approval of the dean of the university, Dr. Arthur H. Larsen. Permission was granted and I spent a good part of the summer with my nose in a book, or working in a laboratory.

One of the courses was Plant Physiology, taught by Dr. Lamke. There were only five or six students in the class, so we had a chance to visit with our department head every day. In many ways, this was as interesting and refreshing as the subject matter in the course.

One day, he told me that there was an opportunity for a graduate student to do some research, and he thought that I might like to take advantage of it. The Illinois Natural History Survey, headquartered in Urbana, had a branch laboratory on Lake Chautauqua, which was near Havana.

The director, Dr. William C. Starrett, was willing to accept a graduate student who was willing to work and who had an interest in Limnology. He would like for me to go with him to meet Dr. Starrett and see if we could arrange a work schedule that would enable me to do the field research for my thesis. He had spoken to Dr. Starrett and told him something about my background of education and experience. The physics, chemistry, and geology courses that I had completed were a big factor in my favor.

Dr. Lamke and I drove to the lab for a Saturday meeting with Dr. Starrett and I was favorably impressed with Dr. Starrett and the program that he recommended. I was also introduced to Frank Bellrose, a specialist in the study of migratory waterfowl. Over the months and years, these two men became my highly respected, dearest friends.

Eventually, I produced a fairly respectable thesis, and after another two or three years of work, a published paper, co-authored by Dr. Starrett, who finally had become Bill, and who was as proud as I was of our work.

I was awarded the degree of Master of Science in Education from Illinois State Normal University in August, 1953.

Dr. Lamke, Frank Bellrose, and Bill Starrett were three who made the angels smile for what they did for me.

That was not the entire story of 1953. Two of our elementary schools in Lincoln were in such bad physical condition that replacement was mandatory. They were too far gone for repairs, so the voters kindly passed a referendum to finance the new building on the site of the old Washington School, and which would also replace the old Monroe School, combining the two districts under one roof, and naming the new building the Washington-Monroe School.

The superintendent and the school board had explained all of the plan to the public, so that, through the cooperation of the *Lincoln Evening Courier,* everyone knew what was going on, and why. Consequently, there was no jealousy or hard feelings in the meshing of the two districts. By the fall of 1953, most of the new building was completed and classes could begin on time.

The faculty, of course, was the combination of the two original districts. Neither of the two principals, however, wanted to be the principal of the new school. I had not given the matter any thought because it was none of my business. We had people who were responsible for such things and I was willing to let them make the decisions. Our Kenny would be attending that school, and I was glad to have it in the district where I lived, but my concerns stopped there.

I was wrong. One morning, Mr. Augspurger called me in and asked me if I would like to be the principal of the Washington-Monroe school. I hesitated before answering, but then he said, "We would like for you to take it." When he said "we" I remembered that the school board had met the night before and I reasoned that the matter had been discussed there.

My answer was loud and clear. "Sure, I'd like that."

From then on, I was on or in that building every day. The foreman was in it to, but there were a few things that came close to getting by both of us. One little problem was that the urinals in the boys restroom in the kindergarten and lower grade part were about chest high to those pupils. The workers pointed out that was what the blueprint called for. The urinals were lowered.

The white tile ceiling blocks in the main hallway were beautiful, except for one box that was off color . . . a kind of sickly yellowish tinge. I was told that they couldn't be changed because the number on the box was the same as the others. I just said ok and went home. After dinner, I went back and using a broom handle, punched a hole through each off-color tile. They were all replaced by the time I made my next visit.

By September, we were ready for classes. I taught the fifth grade because that room was the nearest to the office. It also had a telephone so that I didn't have to leave my class to take calls. Even so, I had to leave my class occasionally. There were not many interruptions, but there were a few. You adjust to them, or go crazy.

The faculty was the greatest. If they even suspected that I wanted or needed something, someone produced it. If something was not right, they fixed it. That school ticked like a fine clock, and I was very proud of my teaching staff.

The children were well-behaved, most from good, solid families. Under less capable teachers, some may have been a small problem. After all, they were young *and* alive!

The parents were helpful, responding readily to parent-teacher meetings, keeping watch over children walking home from school, and occasionally, just sticking their heads in the door to say, "Howdy, is everything all right?"

There came a day when we could say with some pride that the school is finished. Except for one thing: we wanted to have a nice program on our stage in the gymnasium but there was no curtains. Money too short to buy them that year.

At our next teacher's meeting, I explained the situation, and asked if anyone thought that we could do anything about it. Then someone spoke up: "How about an ice-cream social and open house to look over the whole new building?"

The idea caught on, the children sold tickets, the ice-cream dealers furnished ice cream, the school board kicked in the money we lacked, and we had beautiful curtains. They are still hanging there (at the time of this writing), a tribute to the faculty and staff of Washington-Monroe school.

I was the first principal of the Washington-Monroe School. There have been others, and other teachers, as well. They have a tradition to uphold, and I know they will do it, because as I write this, Mrs. Rebecca Cecil is the principal and I know her well. She is my grand niece, by marriage, and the school is in good hands. "Uncle Hab" said so.

My life as a part of Lincoln was nearing an end, but one more event, very important to me, was yet to come: the corn belt council. Boy Scouts of America bestowed upon me the Silver Beaver Award, the highest honor that can be paid to an adult. I will treasure it all the days of my life.

Suddenly, or so it seemed to me, spring had arrived in Central Illinois, school would soon be out for the summer, and I was going to have a little time to catch up on some odd jobs at home and the

Boatman place and still have time for more work on Lake Chautauqua before finally taking another trip west, this time clear to the Pacific, which we had never seen.

One Sunday afternoon we were surprised to see a strange car park in front of the house. It was Dr. and Mrs. Lamke. We were surprised but delighted to see them, and assumed that they were just out for a beautiful spring day drive and had dropped in to say hello. An assumption, which was, at least, partly true.

We sat on the front porch and visited, for the first time, informally and not restrained in any way by teacher-pupil barriers, although I had never been conscious of any restraints in the years I had known these folks.

Finally, Joy mentioned that she had a meal that was ready, and asked if they could stay for dinner. They could, and for a couple of hours past that! Finally, they said that they must be going, that they had enjoyed the visit, and they thanked Joy for the good meal. Mrs. Lamke said, "Father, aren't you going to tell Harry what you came for?" I was surprised, but not really alarmed.

"Well, Harry, Blanch McAvoy is retiring and I have been searching for a replacement. I have several possibilities in mind, all with good credentials, but lacking in variety. I have decided that I would like to have you, if you would be willing."

I could not even dream of replacing Blanche McAvoy. She was known all over the state for her ability as a teacher, especially in the preparation of elementary school teachers for teaching science at that level with a minimum of equipment and formal instruction.

Dr. Lamke noticed my hesitation, then said he knew I was well-fixed here in Lincoln, and that it would be much to give up. He asked me to think it over and talk to my superintendent before coming to see him. He asked if Wednesday would be enough time.

It would. The school board was to meet on Tuesday, and I would know whether they really wanted to keep me or not.

Joy was very careful not to say anything that might influence me in any way, but I was certainly considering her and Kenny. Dr. Lamke had mentioned a figure for salary that gave me a basis for negotiation, so I decided to get it on the floor by going to Mr. Augspurger the first thing Monday morning.

The school board agreed to my request, with the exception of one member. The details came to me within a half hour after the meeting. The dissenting member said, "Harry has this nice new school, a fine staff of teachers, his house is paid for, he lives close to work, and all of his ties are here. He won't leave."

He convinced enough of the members to say no. One member especially, saw the opportunity for me to advance professionally. So, when he got home and had thought about it, he put his hat on again, came over to my house and said, "Harry, take it."

I went to the campus on Wednesday, and come home with the rank of instructor in the department of biological science.

I had been sitting quietly on my own (and paid for) front porch one day, in a mental turmoil of what-to-do-next problems. We decided to solve the problems one at a time, and not to sell the house until we were back from our trip west. I did some more work at the lake and on the house, then made our plans for a real vacation.

Kenny was twelve, just right to be interested in what we would see, and of course, both he and Joy were good campers. We had a good umbrella tent, a homemade muslin tent designed and made by Joy for cooking and eating. Joy had made three sleeping bags with goose feather and down stuffing. We had a Coleman two-burner camp stove and gasoline lantern, and I had converted a large wooden box into a receptacle for cooking gear and a few camping tools. Groceries were carried in cloth bags, and everything we needed could be carried in the trunk of our Studebaker Land Cruiser. Kenny usually rode in the back seat with whatever we needed to reach in a hurry.

The Black Hills, Glacier Park, Yellowstone, Washington wheat fields, the Columbia River, and the Oregon forests, where we visited with Joy's aunt and her family, and then headed home. We were gone almost five weeks, during which it seemed we had a lifetime of pleasure.

My nephew, Kenny Cecil, wanted to buy our house, which pleased me very much. We went house-hunting in Normal. Dr. Ries, who was very glad that we were coming to the biology department, gave us a couple of leads on older homes (that I think were for sale by friends of his), but, instead, we found a newly constructed, two bedroom home in a new addition. I hadn't closed on the sale of our Lincoln house yet, so I needed five thousand dollars, right now, because there were other people trying to buy it. I had never stepped inside the bank in Normal. I knew no one there, and they didn't know me.

I inquired about who was the loan officer and told him I needed five thousand dollars. Instead of the run-around that I expected, he said, "For how long?" and reached for his book of blank notes. I about fell over. We did business with Mr. White and the bank for many years. Oh, yes, I paid the note within the thirty days, as agreed, and my credit was established. Dr. Ries was a little "put out" that we didn't buy one of the houses that he had recommended, but he got over it.

We settled in quickly and comfortably. Our neighbors were friendly, middle class, mostly professional people, business-owners, G.E. executives, teachers, and one wildcat oil man, who, as usual, eventually went broke, and moved out. The last account I had of him, he was back in business. Those boys don't know the meaning of the word quit.

In September, I got my feet wet in college-level teaching. I learned very quickly how to say, "I don't know" and "as far as we know at this time." It is amazing the questions that a good sharp college freshman can ask their teacher. Especially, when you are teaching in a college that requires that they be in the top ten percent of their graduating class for enrollment.

I spent most of my teaching time with freshmen and sophomores in science classes designed for elementary teachers. It was fun to teach and, I hope, courses that would be of value when they were in their own classroom.

I did not use or look at any other's teacher's notes for these classes, but I did rewrite the syllabus for the university catalogue, making room for some of my own pet methods. No one complained, and I finished the first semester having taught essentially the same material that had been taught for years. For the next semester, I had my feet on the ground, and a great many changes were made. The students could throw away their copies of old exams. Life was a new game.

Every day was a new adventure, and every term was an opportunity to make a difference. As I gradually moved up to teaching upper-class subjects, constantly polishing the course content and/or the method of presenting it, some of the professors, who at times taught these courses, thought that there was a danger of losing the course objectives. I did not agree. The whole scientific world was being turned upside down and we had to either change with it or be destroyed by it.

My good friend, Andreas Paloumpis, who also worked at the Havana Lab while I was there, had completed his doctoral studies and joined the faculty. We shared the same office, and one of the first things that we decided was that the less we said, the better off we were. It was amusing to see new faculty telling how much they knew, especially when the president or the dean was within hearing range.

One day, one of my freshman students raised the question of whether we would ever get to the moon or not. I said that there were some problems to solve, and for example, talked about how heavy space vehicles would have to be, and how much force it would take to get the speed essential to get past the gravity limit. Then, I said that I thought we would someday be able to do that. I should have stopped right there, but instead, I added that it might not be in our lifetime!

Within two days, the Russians had *Sputnik* in orbit. Win a few; lose a few!

With the help of countless scientific journals and physics textbooks, I finally gleaned enough knowledge of the space program to help the students understand some of the bare fundamentals.

I remember this particular class very well, partly because it was my first class of full-time college students, but there were other factors. The class met at eight o'clock A.M., but they were wide awake, always pleasant to be with, and dressed as neatly as any group I'd ever had. The women, especially, had a little jewelry to set them off, their hair done neatly, and when you walked into the classrooms, you immediately thought, *ladies*. There were five or six *gentlemen*, too.

I enjoyed them and admired them, and when time came for their first quiz, the papers that I graded amazed me. I could find no fault. I had to give nearly all of them an A.

I took a copy of the test and the papers to the biology office, and said to Dr. Lamke, "Would you please look at this test and the papers? I am new at this business and I think I didn't make my test difficult enough. I would like your opinion." Dr. Lamke looked at the test first, and said, "I'd hate to have to take it." Then, looking at two or three of the papers, he smiled, handed them back to me and said, "If they earn an A, give them an A." So, I did. That was the most delightful class that I ever taught.

Early in the second semester, the university held an "honors day" assembly, acknowledging those students who were on the Dean's List, that is, those with an A average the prior semester. In those days, the faculty attended the assembly whether they wanted to or not. When I walked into the auditorium, there on the stage was every one of the freshmen from my science class.

I have often thought about what I would have done to those fine young people if I had followed the rule of the "normal curve" and deprived them of a well-deserved reward. That time, I think that the angels smiled on *me!*

There were three or four members of the biology faculty that were teaching the various classes required for elementary teachers, so, once a class is completed, it is unlikely that you ever see those students again. That was true of this class, too. The next time I saw any of them was at their commencement four years later. At that commencement, one young lady brought her parents to me and introduced them. Her father took my hand, and with tears in his eyes, said, "We wanted to thank you for all you did for our daughter." That was only the second time that I had that tribute paid to me.

There was one factor, above all others, that made it easy for me to adapt to university-level teaching. That was the cooperation and help that I got from Joy and my son, Kenneth. I knew that it would not be easy for them to leave their home and friends; it never is for anyone. Kenny was just entering junior high, at twelve years old, and that is a difficult time at best. Years later, his little seven-year-old informed his mother, in a moment of pique, "It's not easy being a kid!"

It wasn't too bad until he went to school the first day, and came home ready to explode. It seems that the program of classes was fine, but every pupil was assigned, in addition to their core classes, to either music or art. Kenny had been put in a music section, and he hated it. He couldn't sing at all. He had tried, but just couldn't carry a tune. I believe that I am safe in saying that today, nearly fifty years later, he still can't!

I don't know what arrangements were made, but a little later, he was transferred to the art section, he had made a friend or two, and the world looked brighter.

He soon began to set his sights on University High School and once he got squared away there, he realized what a great advantage he had.

Joy wanted to complete her education, but was reluctant to resume classes until Kenny was through high school. She finally enrolled, and completed her bachelor's degree with a major in Home Economics and a minor in Biology. She completed her Master of Science in Education degree the same year that Kenny graduated with his bachelor's degree. I was one of the happiest men alive that day—a wife and son graduating, and Dad in the faculty line of march. The university photographer, my friend, Nelson Smith, took our picture and I treasure it.

I enjoyed teaching, and in the years that followed, tried to get one freshman class assigned to me, but the university was changing drastically. It had to, and there were reasons why.

In the first place, Dr. Lamke had retired and gone back east to live with his daughter and her family. I kept in touch with him for several years (mostly by Christmas card) and it was a sad day when I received a letter from his daughter saying that he had died.

The chair was filled by a fine man, Omar Rilett, who soon made some changes.

First, Illinois State Normal University no longer served as its true title suggested. This school was really a college. It had only one college; the college of Education. That was its purpose, and for many years, it fulfilled its obligations to the State of Illinois and to its students. It also had a relatively small enrollment. At the time I went there, it was only about twenty-five hundred, with a correspondingly small faculty.

Then, the surge of young people started, fueled, of course, by the advent of the G.I. Bill. I know about this because I was one of them.

It did not happen overnight, but eventually, we had several colleges on the campus; Arts and Sciences, Education, Health and Physical Education and so on. I think that all of the colleges offer Master's Degrees and many, if not all, the Doctorate.

Instead of an enrollment of twenty-five hundred, it now is in excess of twenty thousand, with new dormitories and classroom buildings bulging at the seams.

The faculty is not only larger by far, but are the pick of the teaching and research crop. Great names in many fields are common in the newsletters and catalogues.

It is, as it has always been, a symbol of greatness, and a tribute to our state and to the nation. I am so grateful to have had a hand in its development.

It is now, and has been for some time, Illinois State University at Normal.

Of course, I, as well as everybody else, was affected by these changes. I still taught some of the Biology sections, and my lectures were given in a theater-type room, with 300 seats and sometimes a row across the back to take care of the overflow. While I lectured, two graduate student assistants took the roll. I had three sections, each section met three times a week. I taught nine lectures to over 1000 students, and that just for Biology 100. Other profs had the labs as I taught other courses, too. Frequently, I taught off-campus extension courses requiring travel time, often as far as seventy or more miles. The odd part is, I loved it!

There was one more phase of my academic career that I was drafted for, but which I loved, though the work and mental strain was almost too much.

Like any other good school, Illinois State, especially the College of Education, was highly diversified, and drew freely upon the expertise of faculty members in other colleges and other applicable interests. This practice was exemplified by a situation that arose in or about 1939 when some of the leaders in community affairs saw a need for summer camping programs in McLean County and approached the university regarding some type of training program that would alleviate the shortage of competent counselors and directors.

The end result, approved by President Raymond Fairchild, was to grant credit for those students completing the course,

The McLean County Association for the Crippled agreed to underwrite the course by providing funds for the rental of the Boy

Scout Camp (Camp Heffernan), all expenses paid for counselers and campers.

A university staff member was appointed to direct the project as part of his regular duties during the regular university Post Session, which followed the academic summer session.

Like any major development, there has to be time for reorganization and growth. Eventually, the camp came to be financed by Easter Seals, except for the university staff director who was paid by the university.

The camp was directed by Dr. Cliff E. Horton, head of the Physical Education Department, and the college student counselors earned three semester hours in Health and P.E. credit. The course eventually came to be offered especially for Special Education students, but any junior or senior student was eligible to attend.

I had been on the staff of the Biological Sciences department for several years, and also had attended the University of Illinois summer session to begin piling up credits toward a doctorate degree. I had known Dr. Horton for several years, even before I came to the university to teach. He had been active in scouting, and like me, had been awarded the Silver Beaver, or so I was told. He never mentioned it, or any of his other awards and exploits, which were numerous.

One day, I got a phone call from the dean's office. Dean Larsen needed to see me. What could I have done now? I got the same feeling you get when you are called to the principal's office in high school.

He told me that Dr. Horton wanted to begin breaking in a replacement for the directorship of the McLean County Easter Seals Camp for the Physically Handicapped. Dr. Larsen, Dr. Horton, and President Bone had unanimously agreed that I was the one for the job. I didn't need to be told that there wasn't any question about whether I would accept or not. I got the wheels to turning in my head and couldn't think of one single thing that I could do or say to get out of it. So, I said something silly, like "I'll do my best," and then said, finally realizing the enormity of the assignment, that I appreciated their consideration and I hoped that I would be up to it.

Then, he said, "Thank you for coming over." Now, the president wanted to see me. He asked his secretary to check if Dr. Bone could see me then. He could. He thanked me for accepting such a big job (as if I had a choice) and said he would appreciate it if I would assist "Pop" Horton in any way I could.

I said that I would. He said he would call "Pop" right away and tell him, and that they were all indebted to me.

How could you ever refuse men like that anything they asked for? I happened to know, however, that one of them could be as hard as nails when he needed to be.

I was given the title Director of Counseling Services and went to work, and for seven years, worked with the greatest assortment of college students that I have ever known, the most lovable children, and a great senior staff, which consisted of Charlotte Kohler, RN, camp nurse; William T. Muhl, waterfront director; Dale Spurgeon, counselor for men and boys; Joanne Spurgeon, counselor for girls and women; and Edith Shelton, dietitian. Of course, until he retired, Pop Horton was a giant among any group. Certainly, if angels smiled at the good things people have done for me, this group made them laugh out loud!

I retired from teaching in 1973 and the camp was passed to my good friend, Archie Harris. It was only after I had been retired for a few years that I stopped having nightmares, wondering what I had forgotten to do to get ready for camp. The mechanics and emotional relationships that are a part of such a camp cannot be told here. It would take another book. Suffice it to say, thanks for the memories.

When I was teaching and was principal at Washington-Monroe in Lincoln, we decided to have our annual meeting of the I.S.U. Alumni Club in the new building. Mr. Francis Wade was the director of alumni relations, had taught an extension course in Lincoln, and knew several of us very well. On the night of the meeting, the state car pulled up at the curb and we were surprised to see that Dean Larsen had come with Mr. Wade. I was especially pleased because Mr. Larsen had been helpful in changing the meeting time of some of the on-campus evening courses, so that the Lincoln teachers could attend them. I made it known among some of those teachers that they should express their appreciation in some way, even though I had been the spokesman.

After the program, I took the men on a short tour of the building, the grade placement, and some of the plans for the future. I didn't know at that time that there wasn't going to be any future there for me, but that I would be on the other end!

After I went to the university, I went with Mr. Wade to many alumni meetings.

At the time I was canoe-tripping with the Lincoln boys, I would take my camera and when we had the first PTA meeting I would show slides for the parents. They seemed to enjoy them a lot, so I put together a program of slides and called it *Canoeing Through the Land of Lincoln.*

One time that I gave the program, Dean Larsen was with us. I noticed that he paid close attention, but thought nothing of it.

It was early in the fall, right at that time of year when you want to be outdoors every minute that you can before winter comes. It was only two or three days after the alumni speech that I had another call from the dean's office. Now, I must admit that I was getting a little bit apprehensive about those calls from the dean. It was a short meeting, but pleasantly surprising.

"Harry, would it be possible to take a canoe trip, with five or six faculty men? Just one night out?"

"Yes, that would be easily arranged. The Illinois River has some good scenery for this time of year, and easy places to put in and take out without having to work too hard."

"I have discussed this with these men, and you may want to select someone. We will meet here, and go over your recommendations."

We met, as planned. Pop Horton knew a butcher who could provide us with choice T-bone steaks, Andy Paloumpis and John Sealock tossed a salad, and so on. Believe me, half the fun was in the planning. The time set was for the first weekend after homecoming. The original crew other than those already named was Dr. "Deak" Gooding, head of the Physical Science department, Wally Miller, Biology, and Robert Bone, President.

Those outings (we took four or five) were some of the most enjoyable I ever had. School was never mentioned. Neither were any of our plans made known outside our little circle. The only time the trips were ever mentioned was at an evening of visiting and looking at pictures later in the fall.

I believe that Andy Paloumpis and I are the only ones left.

Family Travels

When I was a youngster, without a playmate a good part of the time, I had lived a very dangerous and exciting life. I finally lost track of all the times I had crashed my (homemade) plane into a mountainside (straw stack), or how many times I had been caught by an avalanche (more straw from the same stack) and had to dig out, or had to dam the stream (broken tile in the pasture drainage system) to make a lake to provide water in times of severe drought for the ranch cattle.

I eventually became addicted to good books, mostly western, and learned to live my adventures vicariously. I had a lot of help with such writers as Jack London, Zane Grey, Owen Wister, Harold Bell Wright, and James Oliver Curwood, along with Helen Hunt Jackson and Gene Stratton Porter (Geneva Porter). These were my favorites, but I would read anything that had a lot of action in it. I even had a go at the Bible. Many years later, I finally did read it cover to cover, but this first attempt ended in disaster. I got along fine, until the verse that tells of Jesus coming into Jerusalem and sending the man for the burro.

That was fine reading, but the King James version that I was reading used a different translation than they do now and it said, "Jesus came riding into Jerusalem on his ass."

That was too much. I burst out laughing. I guess I laughed too long and too hard, because when Dad found out what I was laughing at, he descended on me like a thunderstorm. Suddenly, it wasn't funny any more. I never have seen another New Testament that said it just that way, but I haven't spent much time looking either.

I believe that I must have been born with the lust for adventure and the exploring of the unknown. However, no one ever told me that the work of finding answers only uncovers more questions, and that sometimes you end up feeling more ignorant than when you started. I am sure, though, that the reading that I did as a kid added fuel to the fire, and I have never tired of going and looking, which leads to seeing and feeling.

Fortunately, Kenny had a mother with some of the same ideas. Between the two of us, the kid just had to say yes when Mary Evelyn Donham, a high-school English teacher asked if he would like to go to Alaska for the summer to help her prove up on a homestead that she had acquired. She also had another boy and a young lady Physical Education teacher with her. Of course, when Ken broached the subject at home, Joy and I were about as anxious for him to go as he was.

Ken was seventeen that summer, mature and reliable. He bought an 8mm Mauser rifle at the Army Supply Store, and I believe that was all of the extra equipment he needed. He was an old hand at camping under most any kind of conditions. Canoe-tripping does that to you. He always seemed to have money for the things he needed, as he nearly always had a job of some kind. He could do, and would do, nearly any kind of work.

He and the other boy drove Miss Donham's pickup truck and the ladies drove a car.

We received letters frequently, and they made our mouths water. The seed had been sown for the following summer, when Joy and I thought in terms of the three of us going if we could arrange my work and education schedules for it. We could, and we did.

Of course, we had to camp. There was no way we could afford such a trip if we had to pay restaurant and motel bills every day for four or five weeks. We also invested in a thirteen foot Nomad camp trailer. It had sufficient room for three or four and was superior to a tent in hard rains or clouds of mosquitoes.

I traded cars to get what I wanted: a stick shift, V-8, 1936 four-door. It worked.

We spent many weekends shaking down and experimenting. I didn't want to be stuck two thousand miles from home because of something that I should have checked out before we left. The experiences that Ken had helped us a lot to ensure a trouble-free trip, and when the time finally arrived for us to leave we had light hearts. We also had heavy carpet lashed over the gasoline tank and insulation covering the gas line to protect them from rocks that were picked up by the tires and thrown with great force. Later, when we were nearer to the unpaved road, we also covered the headlights.

The gravel used in Illinois consisted of practically every kind of rock that I ever heard of, but they were from glacial age deposits and creek beds that had been exposed to running water since the continental ice age and had become water-worn and rounded. Consequently, they were not as likely to be picked up by tires as the Canadian rock of the Alaska Highway, which were crushed rock with sharp edges and points that could be thrown with great force.

We had our routine pretty well established. We had done enough camping on weekends to learn the best procedures for a safe camp, not pulling a trailer into any place that you couldn't see a way out of, and fixing tasty, nutritious meals and comfortable beds.

Sometimes, I had said to prospective campers that three people is a bad arrangement for camping. I had observed that there was nearly always a tendency for two to buddy-up, leaving out the third. That was never a problem for Joy, Ken and me. Each had a job, did it, then went on to the next. No one rested until we were all ready, and we didn't know any other way.

Our first mile told us a story: our trailer swayed crazily. I knew what the problem was, I had decided to take a few books along and at the last minute, put them under the bed in the back of the trailer. When I moved them to the front, the sway stopped and we had no more problems until we were cruising along in northern Iowa over a very rough concrete road. We hit one chuck hole too hard and broke a spring leaf on the trailer.

We stopped in two or three little towns, but no one could fix it. We got to Lincoln, Nebraska, before we found a man who replaced the broken spring leaf, then reinforced the other spring, and sent us down the road, greatly relieved but wondering about just how smart we were to undertake such an adventure. The worst was not over.

We ran smack-dab into one of the worst rainstorms I had ever tried to drive in. We could only see a few yards in front of the car and headlights only reflected back into your eyes. We had been watching for a state park that Joy had located on the map, and suddenly, she saw the sign. We soon saw the sign for the campground entrance, and pulled in. We couldn't find a campsite, so I finally saw what I thought was a wide spot in the driveway, and pulled over, hoping I had cleared enough room for other cars to pass.

For a while, we just sat in the car, but finally, we decided to make a break for the trailer. We did the right thing. Even though we got soaking wet, we had a good supper, a good night of sleep, and no let-up in the rain until the morning. The next day was very pleasant, and we enjoyed the trip immensely.

I remember saying that the scenery we were seeing was so great that I doubted if we were going to see any much better. Wrong again. On the way home five weeks later, I asked why anyone would vacation there.

We didn't have any trouble crossing the border, the border officials were courteous and helpful and asked only pertinent questions like, "Do you have sufficient funds?" We hoped we did. We enjoyed Regina, impressed by the cleanliness that is so characteristic of Canadian towns and cities.

Saskatchewan and Alberta have, along with huge grain elevators, wide areas of forests and mountains which are a drastic contrast to the flat grass prairie that we were accustomed to.

At Edmonton, we stopped long enough to go to a bank to have some of our money changed, and from there on to mile 0 of the Alaska Highway at Dawson Creek, British Columbia, where I changed the oil and gave the car a good grease job and general check-up. I had checked the oil daily as we drove north, but hardly expected to drive as far as Dawson Creek without having to add more. My faith in the little Chevrolet was justified. I did have to add one quart before we got home, but that was all. Steady driving at fifty miles per hour seemed to be the answer. Our gasoline mileage so far was slightly more than fourteen miles per gallon.

From here on, our "steady driving" came to an end. There was just too much to see. The road was blacktop for about thirty miles, and then, gravel. There were plenty of chuck holes, so our speed was diminished, but who wants to speed through scenery like we were seeing? There were several, for example the great semi-milk trucks bound for Anchorage or Fairbanks and many places in between. Trucks left the dairy country and headed north, non-stop, except for fueling and change of drivers and making their delivery within twenty-four hours. Give them plenty of room to pass; they need it and will take it.

There were accommodations about every thirty miles, and they served good food and made good rest stops. Of course, we did not need overnight accommodations, but we rarely passed one without stopping.

On and on we drove, the names of places that I had read about and that Ken had seen the summer before, sounded like music to Joy and me. Watson Lake, Teslin, the Laird River and finally, Whitehorse, a major stop for us to explore in order to get our first good look at the Yukon River and to really stand on the soil of the Yukon Territory. Sometimes, dreams do come true!

Probably the high point of the day for us was the finding of some of the decommissioned paddle wheel steamboats that had been used in gold rush times to haul passengers and freight on the Yukon River. Two of them were still in pretty good condition, and one of them, the *Klondike*, was safe enough to go aboard and explore. This experience alone was enough to justify the trip to see it. The paddle wheel steamers were, in my opinion, one of the great achievements of mankind, not only because of its freight and passenger carrying capacity, but as a work of art and stimulating beauty.

From Haines Junction north to Snag, the St. Elias Mountains occupied our attention and we found ourselves stopping to just stand and look about as much time as we spent driving.

Finally, at milepost 1221, we entered Alaska and could stand on property that originally had been purchased for five cents an acre. About eighty miles farther up the road, we came to Tok and the customs stop. You would have thought that we were bringing half of Canada with us, but we were finally on our way again, and at Mile 1523 we were in or near Fairbanks.

We felt as if we were living in a different world, and indeed, we were. Here, we could look and feel and touch almost as if you were living in some kind of dream world, and we loved it. We also knew that we had to pick and choose, because any one of the places that we planned to visit could occupy our attention for weeks if not months.

Of course, we had planned to visit with Miss Donham at her homestead where she had established a café and Ken and John had built a small log cabin for hunters. She had written, saying that she would appreciate some help putting in a gasoline tank, as she was between Fairbanks and the distant Early Warning Station at Clear on the Tanana River. We were glad to help her and it would give us an opportunity to do something besides ride in a car.

She lived on a pretty good road for those times in Alaska, but as we drove out of Fairbanks, we noted some curves with drop-offs on one side that could, under the right conditions, make your hair stand on end!

We were made very welcome at Donhams Café and were especially relieved to see that the hole had been dug for the tank by some high-school boys.

The next day, Ken and I went into Fairbanks to get the tank. We used Miss Donham's truck, a pick-up with a short bed. I wished many times that I had arranged for a different truck! We had to lash the front of the tank to the truck as the tank stuck out behind more than half its length, taking a good deal of weight off the front wheels. On the way home, when we came to a sharp curve, I had to speed up a little, then as I turned, apply the brakes gently to give the front wheels traction enough to follow the road.

To say that we were glad to get home was putting it mildly.

The next day, I backed the truck up to the hole, placed some poles over the hole, and dropped the tank down on the poles. Good shot. Now, we had to drop the tank down into the hole with the pump connections exactly vertical. We removed all but two of the poles, then each taking a sledge simultaneously knocked the poles apart, dropping the tank exactly where we wanted it.

The high school boys filled the hole, somebody did the electrical work, and Miss Donham was in the oil business.

We were glad to see the log cabin that Ken had helped build. Not everyone has had the opportunity for that experience, even though the logs were pre-cut. It was small, but ideal for its purpose.

Ken had one other unusual experience that summer. There was no indoor (or outdoor, either) plumbing on the Donham homestead. Water had to be hauled from a spring about thirteen miles away, therefore, toilet facilities consisted of an outhouse some distance from the café.

One day, the womenfolk were in the outhouse at a time when a black bear came angling by and took up a station effectively preventing the women from returning to the café, or going any other place, either. I believe that Ken had told Joy and me that the bear had caused some problems around there before, a common problem where there are people and the smell of good food.

The girls called to Ken and John to get the gun. Ken got his Mauser and shot the bear. The meat was given to some needy folks, and Ken took his place with Daniel Boone. Ken didn't carve KILLED

A BEAR on a tree as Boone did, and I think that Ken did not really enjoy the experience. At least, the killing part.

It is fifty-eight miles from Fairbanks to Nenana and the café was near the halfway point between the two. Ken wanted us to visit Nenana and see the Tanana River and perhaps the DEW station at Clear. We enjoyed the drive in that area as we saw several Indian homes and one "fish camp." The Tanana River is wide, deep and fast. We could see that anyone who fell into the river would be lost and the possible truth in a story that I heard some place, but have forgotten where. It seems that it required a fairly large group of workers for the loading or unloading of supplies necessary for the construction of the DEW station. Indian workers with money in their pockets would come to work drunk, and many of them fell into the river and drowned. To prevent these alcohol-related incidents, the managers instituted the buddy system, such a procedure as used by boy scouts. Today, you work, and I get drunk; tomorrow I work, and you get drunk. I suppose the plan succeeded. I never heard a report.

We had decided that we would stop on the way back to Fairbanks and buy some fish at a camp we had seen. We found it and saw an Indian woman sitting on a bench with a can of beer in her hand and enough empty cans in a pile to fill the bed of a pick-up. A sign said FRESH FISH, and there was a rowboat hauled up onto high ground and loaded to the gunwales with fish, and flies.

The woman came up to the car as we were getting out, and said, "This my fish camp. My son he work here. It my fish camp. I call my son. He work here."

The son came up to us, greeted us, and, when asked, stated that he did indeed have fresh fish down at the fish wheel. He had noticed me looking at the boat full of fish, smiled, and said, "Those are to be dried for winter dog food." I was relieved.

"How many do you want?"

"How big are they?"

"Oh, they're not very big."

"Well, I guess three will be enough."

Soon he came back carrying three of those "not very big" fish. I had been thinking in terms of one each for supper. The smallest one measured thirty-two inches; they weighed about ten or twelve pounds each. He charged two dollars each for them.

We had Coho salmon for supper. It was good. We had the others on ice, so we headed for Valdez, eating salmon the next day, and also the next. All the same fish.

I was beginning to look for a hungry dog when we pulled into a parking lot for campers at Valdez. I told Joy to leave the skillet in the drawer, we were going to eat something besides salmon.

We saw a small crowd a short distance away, and soon, a man came over to us and asked, "Do you folks by any chance have any fresh salmon?" They were having a church fish fry, had run out of salmon except for some frozen ones.

We fixed him up real good, and refused the frozen ones. I didn't eat salmon for a long time, but for supper that night, I had a seafood dinner at a Valdez restaurant that was the best I had ever eaten. The next morning, we visited the Valdez glacier and looked long at Valdez bay, wishing that we had the time and the money to take a cruise or trips to the dozens of interesting places in this area. We did not go to the salmon cannery. What we did was to spend so much time just *looking* at scenery as beautiful as any in the world. We just wanted to remember all we could because we were reasonably sure that we would never have the opportunity to see it again. It cost us hours of driving time, but we didn't care, and finally we turned back north on the Richardson Highway toward Mt. McKinely and the Denali National Park.

We had planned to be in the vicinity of Mt. Healy in time to see a portion of the caribou migration, which was due to pass there the first or second week in July. The day before the scheduled time, we packed a little grub, sleeping bag, a one-burner alcohol stove to heat tea and soup, and headed for Mt. Healy. We spent some time on the summit then moved down to a shoulder out of the wind to sleep. I was about ten o'clock the next morning before we saw them coming, lazying along as if they had forever to get there. After we watched them for an hour or so, we went close, tried to keep up with them walking, and discovered that the "lazying along" gait required us to run to keep up. It was one of the great awe-inspiring experiences that I have ever witnessed.

I had been taking water samples from some of the tundra ponds to get an idea of the living flora and fauna species present, the relative population density and the possible relation of these organisms to other wildlife of the arctic. One of the small lakes was near the campground and easily accessible.

One morning, I was on my knees dipping water to run through my plankton seine. When I stood to stretch a bit, I found myself looking into the eyes of a cow moose. A young calf standing nearby was apparently as puzzled as its mother.

I said good morning, but she didn't answer. I very cautiously stood up, picked up my gear, and moved over to the path back to camp. The moose ignored me, walked into the water, and began to feed on the submergent vegetation. I watched them for a while and assumed that people were not unknown to her. That must have been true, because she and I shared that collection station for two or three days. When I was working, she and the calf waited in the background. When she was grazing as I arrived, I waited in the background. It was a fine arrangement.

I learned from her that the moose is a beautiful animal, and if they don't want you to hear them move through the forest, you will not hear them. I tried to walk through the growth as quietly as she, but I failed the test. I hope she lived to a ripe old age. I was sorry that I had enjoyed the moose meat loaf that Miss Donham served at the café so much.

Ken had told us that the best place to see Mount McKinley was from Wonder Lake which is about eighty miles from McKinley Park Station. It was not recommended for trailers over sixteen feet long, and we decided that ours could sit there in the camp ground and we would "rough it". We had light tents, one for Ken and one for Joy and me, and other gear for cooking and, of course, sleeping bags.

There is much to see along that little road. It is mostly tundra with an occasional arctic willow and campgrounds from twenty to fifty miles apart. There is a visitor's center at Eielson and a ranger station at Wonder Lake.

We got to see one of the famous Toklat Grizzly bears putting on a show for us, although I doubt if they were interested in spectators. There was a fairly large tree about three hundred or four hundred feet from the road. It was large enough to provide some shade for the beautiful sow that was lying beneath it trying to get a nap. There were two cubs interfering somewhat by climbing the tree six or seven feet high, at which time the limb would bend over, the cub would fall to the ground, and repeat the performance. The cubs were having a wonderful time and I suspect that Mama was, too . . . until one cub landed smack on top of Mama, at which time, a resounding blow with a forepaw sent junior rolling across the tundra for about twenty feet. That ended the game, and we got back in the car and drove on.

The mental image of a bear attacking with teeth bared and forearms ready to administer the famous "bear hug" was largely displaced with a that of a gentle, loving mother playing with her children. I suppose that there has to be room for both.

We hadn't gone far when we saw another denizen of the tundra entertain but this time, for a price.

This one was a red fox, standing as close to the road as he dared without getting hit by a car. He was the strangest looking fox I ever saw. His hair (excuse me, "fur") was tangled and matted, he looked to be half-starved, and his once-bushy tail was a mere stub. His eyes, though, were bright and shiny and I think he was grinning at us because he saw some victims coming to his show.

This old boy was a pan-handler dating clear back to Adam, but what can you do? We have people like that, too, you know.

It has long been a custom in our family to go into the field with an ample supply of food, water, and essential survival gear. On this day, the food consisted of graham crackers, raisins, soda crackers, and I believe I had a small hunk of cheese.

I offered our host a graham cracker. It was gone before I knew what had happened. The same thing happened with the next one, and the next. . . . Then, it was repeated with the raisins, and finally, I had nothing left but soda crackers and neither did Joy or Ken. When I offered a soda cracker, he took it gently, carried it well off the road and buried it, made his rounds with the rest of the family, then just sat and looked at us. Finally, we located the rest of the family, all sitting at the mouth of a den located near the top of a little hill and looking down at us.

He reminded me of an incident the occurred at Miss Donham's. An Indian stopped at the café one day. He was driving a pick-up and was accompanied by his wife and a little boy about three or four years old. The Indian was a nice-looking man, and he visited with Joy and me while he enjoyed a piece of pie and a cup of coffee. He was a trapper in the winter, and worked at whatever he could get to do during the summer. He told us about having to back pack all of his supplies to his winter camp and depend largely on game for food. Then, he said, "Now we have a pilot fly us in, and we think we have to have all kinds of fancy food, like (in a sneering tone of voice) fruit cocktail!" Then, he stood, said that he had enjoyed talking with us, and drove away with the little boy still trying to see out the window. No pie—no coffee for Mama; no candy or chewing gum for the little boy.

How like the little kids! Stoicism is learned early.

Ken and I walked out over the tundra for a short distance, mostly just to get the feel of it. There was a lot of green color in the vegetation, but also enough brown to tan, and even some yellow, making a type of natural camouflage that made good hiding for the Toklat Grizzly bears that frequent this type of habitat. We did not wander far from the car, prefering to see "cute little bears" from a distance.

We arrived at Wonder Lake Campground a little past mid-afternoon, pitched our tents, and visited with other tourists, hoping for the cloud cover to break away from the mountain. No luck. Ken thought that there was no use to watch too closely, as it was not likely that the clouds would be gone before the next morning.

We had become accustomed to the long days and short nights, so it was easy to go to sleep, even though it was full daylight. Some of the tourists stayed awake so they could call the ones who slept, and it was about 2:00 A.M. when a man stopped at our tents and told us that the clouds were disappearing.

We watched toward the south and saw what I thought was Denali becoming visible. Ken said, "No. That is just one of the foothills. As we watched, I became more and more awed by a mountain, fifty miles away, that completely filled the view-finder on the camera. I cannot describe the feeling that I had, and that was shared by everyone there. I'll vouch for one thing. There was not an atheist in that crowd that morning. At least, after the sun exposed Denali. No one was talking; some cried and some prayed. Our mission to Wonder Lake was a complete success. Not everyone is so lucky, and more times than not, the cloud cover keeps the mountain hid.

There was so much to see and do, but we were a long way from home, and time to be headed south. The scenery was just as beautiful, the people we met were just as nice, but we were getting tired of traveling.

I believe it was someplace in Alberta that we had a close call with a car problem. We were cruising along with Ken driving and Joy searching the travel guide for a campsite. She said, "There is one just ahead." I think she said it was about two miles ahead. That sounded good, as we had promised ourselves a good long sleep.

The road was good and we had been driving a little faster than usual. Then we saw the campground sign near the foot of a little hill that we had just topped. Fine, now we could eat and rest . . . except that, instead of slowing down and turning in at the entrance, Ken didn't slow down. In fact, he speeded up.

I remember saying, "Ken, why in hell didn't you stop?"

The answer was simple. "I haven't got any brakes!"

That was the first time that I remembered that when I prepped the car, covering gas tank and lines, headlights and anything else that I thought might be damaged, I completely forgot to protect the brake lines. We had lost our brake fluid. Our question was, "How far can we drive over semi-mountainous terrain without any brakes?" Going downhill with a trailer pushing you from behind? Well, we hoped that there were no high hills and long downhill slopes before we got to a garage, or to someplace where we could call for a new line or to have the old one patched.

Joy had her trusty travel guide, and after a brief study, told us there was a stopping place down the road that had a filling station and garage. We drove in low gear and there was no traffic. There were also three deep-breath sighs of relief when we pulled into the service center.

It was closed for the night, but the man said he could fix it as there was an old Chevy wreck down the road a piece, and he would go get a brake line off it in the morning.

Joy fixed a good supper and daylight or not we went to bed. By eight o'clock the next morning, we had the brake line replaced, new brake fluid installed and the gas tank full. Our bill was twenty dollars! I told the man that wasn't enough, but he wouldn't take more. He said the tourists were nice to him and made him a good living. He would not overcharge just because he could.

The Canadians are great. I wish Americans would keep their garbage and trash in their cars instead of littering *our* highways.

There are many places in our own northern states that are very beautiful, but on the way home, after seeing the western and northern territories of Canada, I wondered why anyone would not be willing to make the trip. Well, I do understand. It takes time and money, and not everyone has that combination of assets.

When we pulled into our driveway, that little old house in Normal looked awfully good.

Back Home Again

Our trip to Alaska was one of the greatest adventures that any family could have, but being home again was also relaxing and comfortable . . . for a while.

We were anxious to make contact with our families. They were anxious to hear from us, as we didn't exactly wear out the postal service with letters while we were gone. I had last-minute jobs to do to get ready for Crippled Children's Camp, preparations for the fall semester, and, of course, the usual maintenance for house, lawn, and car, to say nothing of little tasks that had been saved for me by Joy's parents on the little Hill Farm.

Kenny enrolled at the university, and Joy, who had only taken a course or two, also enrolled full-time, completing her B.S. with a major in Home Economics and a minor in Biology. She also graduated with high honors, and taught high school Home Economics for several years.

Generally, enrollment had begun a rapid increase with the advent of the G.I. Bill, and, adding that to the natural population increase and a better economic environment, was a sure sign of pressure on educational institutions.

The result was an effort to limit enrollment to 6000 students, up from about 2500 when I was a student. Of course, it didn't work, and by 1973, we were rubbing the 20,000 mark and still growing, with corresponding demands on faculty and physical facilities.

It was during this time that some of the far-sighted administrators, especially Bone, Larsen, Rilett (Biology Department Head), started a drive for a name change. I have already mentioned that the name, Illinois State Normal University, was a misnomer because there was only one college. We now had more than one college, in fact, if not on some legal document.

Someone wrote the appropriate document, most faculty read it, and it was submitted to the state legislature and other interested bodies for study. It already had the blessing of the Teacher's College Board of Regents.

Several of us from Biology and Administration attended the State Legislature on the day it was to be presented. I was told that I was needed as I knew some of the legislators, and because I was a graduate, as were my son and my wife, and was also a member of the faculty. It would "look good" if I went.

I was honored to be considered, and was grateful for the chance to represent the faculty at the legislative session.

The name change was approved, and I.S.N.U. became Illinois State University at Normal, or just plain I.S.U. I must admit, however, that we who had been associated with I.S.N.U. for so many yeas could not deny that we were saddened at times at the loss of what used to be.

Almost before I knew it, I realized that I had completed more than seven years at I.S.U. and was eligible for sabbatical leave. I could either take a full year at $1/2$ pay or $1/2$ year at full pay. I elected the $1/2$ year at full pay. I had attended summer school at the University of Illinois, and one semester of work would round out the course requirements for the doctorate.

I enjoyed that summer immensely, with one or two exceptions, and I had no control over them. For example, I needed the course in genetics. The professor that I had waited for finally agreed to teach a summer session course, so I signed up for it. Two days before the term began, he had an accident and the university had to get a substitute. It was some joker from Indiana who was ticked off because he had to lower himself by coming to Illinois for eight weeks.

That old boy made life a living hell for about twenty doctoral candidates. Enough said. I got a C in his section (flunking in a doctoral program), but I got an A in the laboratory section, which raised me to a B for the course. Based on what I learned in the course, I should have repeated it, for genetics is an interesting and necessary field in which every biologist should be proficient. But, I didn't.

Professor Max Matteson and Hobart Smith are two men who will ever stand tall, both as teachers and as gentlemen, and I am sure they made the angels smile more than once.

After the retirement of Dr. Lamke, we had been lucky to get Dr. Omar Rilett to fill the post of Department Head. Two of our department members had been his students and this probably was partially why we were able to get him. He was a man determined to make the department one of the best in the country and he wasted no time in doing just that. He searched for faculty with expertise in fields where we were deficient, one of which was herpetology. The man to fill it was Alan Holman, who had received his doctorate at the University of Florida, and though my own interests were mostly in the field of fresh water aquatics, I had investigated some of the natural history of a small chorus frog native to the Illinois sand prairie, which occurs along some regions of the Illinois River. Al and I became friends and we did some field studies at the sand prairie together. I being familiar with the sand prairie and he with frogs . . . but not this particular species, a small Hylidae *Pseudacris streckeri*. Al got sidetracked by other activities, and the frog problem was continued by Lauren Brown, myself and Lauren's wife, Jill Brown, later.

There was a mutual interest in the ecology of the southwest desert areas and their relationship to the dry areas of north and central Mexico. Al had been in contact with Dr. Hobart Smith, who had been involved some way in the study of the effects of overgrazing in the Mexican desert grasslands as related to the migration of certain plant species from the south to the north. The University of Illinois had been connected in some way to the research, but now would like for Illinois State to carry it on. Al was interested; was I? I was. We could make the essential observations in a few days, and Easter break was the logical time for us to make the trip. We could also take our wives. That was no problem, either.

We came pretty close to a problem, though. There was another man from the University of Florida who wanted to go along. Al didn't want to take him because he was fifty years old and might have a heart attack or something.

I said, "Al, if we take your car, there won't be room!" We took Al's car (which we had planned on anyhow) and that settled the transportation problem. I didn't tell Al that I was not far from fifty, as well!

I knew that this trip was not really going to be a picnic because we had a lot of observations to make, many miles to drive and only about ten days of free time for it. We hurried our preparations of equipment, and checked the car. Joy and Donna put out some food for travel snacks and we were ready.

On the last day of classes, we wished our students a happy Easter vacation and pulled out of our driveway, headed for old Route 66 south. It was cold, the pavements were wet, and we were heading right into a snow storm. Fortunately, the snow didn't amount to much and by the time we reached St. Louis, the weather had cleared. Joy had fried a big skillet full of chicken, and that was our supper, which we ate as we drove along with plenty of bread and butter, and a thermos of coffee. I have a lot of memories from that trip, but one of the most vivid is of Al driving along as if the devil was behind him, with a piece of chicken in one hand, and the steering wheel in the other. Our only stops were at filling stations to fill up and empty out.

"Breakfast at McAlester" became a familiar phrase in future years and trips. One of the nice things about repetitive trips is that you get acquainted with people and find the best places to eat along the way. McAlester had such a place on our route and we always stopped there, both coming and going.

We had lunch south of the Dallas turn-off (we were not on an interstate that had "Exits") then later finished the chicken and the Sloppy Joe's that Donna had made. It was late bedtime when we arrived in Eagle Pass, found the Eagle Hotel, and slept the sleep of the *very* tired.

The next morning, Al bought some Mexican insurance on the car, we changed our money into Pesos, and crossed the border into Mexico and the city of Piedras Negras. The first large sign that you see said FORD GARAGE, but from there on you knew that you were south of the border without signs.

Fortunately for us, the road that we took was an excellent blacktop. I was told that the U.S. had loaned Mexico the money required to build it, and that the debt was paid in full when the loan was due. That's a new twist for our loans. As a citizen of the U.S., I appreciated it. I hope that what I was told was true.

Our main goal was the Bolsom Desert area in the state of Durango, but we took our time to get acquainted with the country as best you can from a car at sixty miles per hour. Too bad, but our time was limited and we had work to do.

Briefly, our route was to go south through Nueva Rosita and Monclova to Saltillo (on Route 57), then west on Route 40 to Torreón and on southwest to Durango and finally to Mazatlan on the Pacific.

We had driven a lot of miles and it was good to be where we could make our observations and collect our samples on our feet.

We had a little problem with the weather. A cold front had moved in and the herptiles (amphibians and reptiles) that we wanted to identify and collect were hiding out someplace where it was warm. In the entire trip, we only saw one iguana, but the Mapimi Indian who was helping us that day told us that large ones were scarce as the natives considered iguana tail a delicacy.

We enjoyed this man, who spoke no English, and neither Al nor I spoke Spanish. It was remarkable that we could communicate at all, but we did pretty well with smiles, body language, grunts, and a few sounds that must have sounded like words. He thought it was very amusing that Al and I had brought some food and a small canteen of water. He said (I think), "We are only going to be out one day!"

The going pay rate for this job was about four or five pesos. I don't know what the exchange rate was at that time, but I remember that Al and I had a guilty conscience (that in itself is worthy of note), about him working for so little, probably about fifty cents per day. We had been cautioned about paying too much, so, we finally compromised by offering to buy him a couple of beers at the cantina. He accepted, and I never saw a bottle of beer emptied so quickly. Likewise, the second and third, and I don't remember how many more. He was a very large man, and we knew that he had earned them. I wish him well.

While Al and I were doing field work, Joy and Donna had gone sightseeing. They inquired at the desk about what there was of interest to them, including the market. The proprietor generously offered them a young girl clerk that he said he could spare for the day.

The young lady took them to the market and some of the stores, then took them to her grandmother's house for tea. They had a wonderful day and I had to wonder how long a Mexican would have to hunt in our country before he found someone who would be so friendly and so helpful.

The next day, Al and I spent in the field again, but finally, gave up hope of getting a specimen of the famous desert tortoise that is extant in that area. When we returned, we ate dinner and decided to go on toward the foothills of the Sierra Madres (occidentalis) and to Mazatlan. Someone told us the buses made the trip in about ten hours.

Well, maybe they do, but we couldn't. Perhaps we did too much looking. There certainly was plenty of beautiful country to see, and the mountains are especially beautiful at that time of year, with large colorful flowers everywhere.

We were following a bus part of the way and were surprised to see it stopped near a bridge over a very deep canyon. Just beyond, we could see a train of people apparently climbing up to meet the bus, and leading a burro. Off in the distance, we could see a village, and apparently, that was the hometown of the people we saw.

The bus door opened as the people came up to it, a lady carrying a tiny baby got out, the people made a great fuss over them, helped them mount the burro, and immediately began the long walk to the village.

This was at a place named Buenos Aires, according to a sign on the bridge. Apparently, it was a bus stop replacing a rest stop. The men went on one side of the bus, the women on the other. It might be "good air" to those folks, but to us the stench was awful. Bless them, they do the best that they can. We arrived at Mazatlan a short time before dark.

There were some very fine-looking hotels, facing the ocean and assorted beach activities, but I had my doubts about them, being as anxious to please us as the folks at Durango were.

Sure enough, when I asked if we could get two rooms for overnight, the answer was a very definite, "no," which is the same word in Spanish as it is in English.

I was going to ask where the nearest Mexican hotel was, but instead I just thought, *To Hell with you, Bud* and went back out doors. We found a hotel just around the corner and down a block, getting rooms for two dollars each. I was the only one that was hungry, so I went down the street to a restaurant, and ordered a Mexican plate that was as good as any I had ever eaten, and went upstairs in the hotel to our room. I saw a man sitting on the steps at the foot of the stairs, but didn't give it any thought until I found that the rooms did not have locks on the doors. He was our guardian angel for the night. After breakfast the next morning, we headed back to Durango as we were running out of time. We all agreed that the drive over the Sierra Madres was well worth the time and effort.

We spent another day in the field, finding very little of value except a couple of snakes representative of a species that we did not have in the university collection. We sacked them up to ride in style on the roof of the little station wagon.

At noon, we stopped at a little restaurant and ordered the meal. It was a cheese sandwich. They had one choice, that was it. In those restaurants, you eat what they have.

I tasted that cheese sandwich and was so surprised I am sure that it showed. I have never eaten cheese as good as that. I saw the menu that was written on a chalk board, but didn't know what it meant. *Queso Cabrito,* cheese made from goat milk, might have scared me off had I known what it meant.

I ordered another. The little sixteen-or-so-year-old waitress turned to a man sitting across the room and laughingly said something to him. He chuckled and said to me, "She said that you must be very hungry!" I told him I thought the sandwich was one of the best I've had, and he said they make their own cheese and it is aged in caves in the lava bed near the little village. He said, "It really is a fine food."

He asked us where we were from and I told him Illinois. He asked if it was any place near Pontiac. I said Bloomington was our main town. He had worked on the railroad for several years and was well-acquainted with the area.

I tipped the waitress generously, then went back to the open desert. The next morning, we headed home.

We had a little trouble at the Border Station with the U.S. boy. He went through the whole car, unloaded everything, threw things around, and made us all as mad as hell.

At last, he reached up and grabbed one of the snake bags off the car, untied the string and as he was ready to reach down into the bag, he said, "And what's in here?"

About that time the rattler buzzed good and loud. He could darn well tell what was in the bag. He handed the bag back to Al, and said, "Get out of here!"

We got back to I.S.U. in time to begin classes again, without much money, but very, very, much richer.

Ken Grows Up

Sometime during the summer of 1964, Joy's folks attended a fair or carnival someplace and Mom Boatman played a game or something. She won a lot in a new development at a place called Woodland Hills at Hardy, Arkansas. Because we had worked so hard to provide a home for them, they had the lot put in Joy's and my name. Good! It sounded like a pretty place to build a cottage and spend a restful old age. I didn't realize at the time that "restful old age" was something like forty years in the future.

Mom Boatman was real proud of what she had done, and when Joy suggested that we take a little trip to Arkansas to see the new property, the folks were all for it.

We saw the potential. The addition was pretty, had a nice lake (under the supervision of the Arkansas Fish and Game folks) and the plans were for rapid improvement as soon as enough lots were sold. Lots adjacent to the one we now owned were selling for fifty dollars each, so I bought two more and then a third, a really beautiful lot, nicely shaded and near the lake, where we thought we really might build a cottage within a year or two. "The best laid plans of mice and men . . ."

A series of events, mostly of my own choosing, led to an entirely different scenario. I got rid of all of the lots, except the one nearest to the lake. Sooner or later, I will decide to do something with it, or give it to somebody. The taxes are $8.65 this year. I guess I can afford to keep it a while longer. At least the dream was not a nightmare!

Ken had graduated from the university and had begun work on his master's degree. He also was finding time to pay some attention to "the little girl next door," although next door was actually one block behind our house which was convenient enough to lead to a serious relationship. We were not surprised when Ken announced one day that he wanted to have a family conference.

The young lady's name was Judith Ann Tindall and they wanted to get married . . . all of which we already knew and approved. They were married on the twenty-first day of August 1965, honeymooned in Colorado, and came home to a little apartment where they were anxious to entertain us for the first time.

They had a davenport backed against the wall, and that was where Joy chose to sit. We were talking and having a nice time, when Joy said, "I smell horse." Everybody laughed, but Ken finally enlightened us. He had been riding a horse at a little stable in Normal. He liked her, wanted her, and bought her. She was a young Standard Bred, broken to ride, but not well-educated. We were glad for them. Joy liked horses as much as I did, but neither of us had ridden for years. That is just the first of a series of incidents, each one triggering the next, that led to a different kind of life for all of us. The horse smell? A horse blanket was stored in the only available space in the apartment ... behind the davenport.

Ken had never had an opportunity to ride and was a little hesitant and strange to the young filly. One day, he asked if we would come to the stable and see what he was doing wrong.

I watched him for a while and thought I had found the source of the problem. There was a problem; Ken was afraid he would hurt her, and he was not at ease.

I suggested that I try her. The horse relaxed and we had a good ride around the little arena track. Ken regained his self-assurance and so did the horse. No more problem. In a short time, he was a good rider and so was Judy.

A few days later, Art, the stable-owner said, "Harry, I have a little horse here that I would like for you to try." Now, I have not been around horse people a good part of my life without learning that one of the ubiquitous habits is to get a green horn on a horse that will buck or do some other silly behavior to embarass the rider ... especially if he is some kind of white-collar worker (like a professor) or a smart-alec kid.

I started to decline, but Art seemed to be on the level. I had work clothes on, and I thought, *Heck, it might be fun to be thrown!* So, I said, "OK, let's go get her."

She was a black mare with some Arab blood, and as pretty as a picture. Art said she belonged to a young girl, but the mare was too much for her and she would sell her for two hundred fifty dollars.

I rode her around the track at walk, trot and canter. She had her own ideas about that. She was spoiled rotten, and thought she could do as she pleased. At one time, she had been well-trained, but she had buffaloed riders since then until no beginning rider could do anything with her.

I proceeded to straighten her out. It took about fifteen minutes to begin an enjoyable ride, but for months, every time I got on her, I had to show her who was riding who.

I bought her and I loved her, but I finally sold her to a girl who loved her and loved to ride her. When she graduated from the university and moved to Missouri, Candy went along.

It was not long after all of this that Judy was at our house about the time that the daily paper was delivered, and she or Joy saw an ad advertising eighty acres of wooded land with some cleared for pasture for sale. I don't know what it was in the ad that caught their eye, but I do know that this was only the beginning of a series of events and circumstances that was going to cost me dearly, both in money and labor. On the other hand, if I had to do it over, making the same responses with the same ultimate cost, I probably would be that foolish again.

First, I said, "Forget it." When the girls decided they would go take a look at it, some sixth sense told me I had lost the first round.

Then, when they convinced me that it was essential that I see it, too, I began to have doubts about the second round.

I might as well have thrown in the towel in the first place. It was a beautiful spot, all hills and valleys except for enough fairly level land that would do for a hay field and a house and barn. What a man won't do for a wife, a daughter-in-law and two horses! On the other hand, I was tired of living in town, *any* town. I wanted a place like this for my retirement years, and, since Joy was teaching now, we didn't have any financial worries. Some concerns, but no worries. We bought it, built a house and barn, had a well dug, built what seemed like a thousand miles of fence, went to school a few summers, and directed the Crippled Children's Camp after Dr. Horton retired.

We built the barn and converted an old brooder house into a tack shed. We pulled our little trailer out there to give us shelter until we had the house ready for us, and worked up the field set aside for hay. I applied lime and fertilizer, worked it into the ground, and sowed a mixture of orchard grass and alfalfa. The plot greened up with beautiful forage soon after a good rain. I only took two cuttings off of it the first year, but three each year after that. That was par for our climate.

Soon after, we saw a good growth in the field. Joy and I walked over it, and in about an hour, returned to the trailer with my hat about half full of arrowheads. Something surely had happened there!

Joy and I built the house with only a few days' help from various people: my niece, Marcie Dougherty, and her husband, Jack, several men from Alpha Phi Omega fraternity (I was the faculty sponsor) among them, Willie Keneller, who married a fine young woman who had been one of my students, and others, whom I can no longer recall.

The only work that I hired someone to do was the tile on the bathroom walls, around the tub. That was the only work that had to be done over. The same man did it, *right* this time.

It took us nearly three years, one board at a time, we would pay the lumber company at the end of each month. Finally, the house was finished, and paid for.

As soon as we had the new house liveable, we put our house in Normal up for sale. It was a cute little house, and a good one, fairly priced. It sold quickly, and we were grateful for that. We certainly didn't need two houses. Now, we had about everything we needed to keep us happy: woods, fields, assorted wild animals such as deer, 'coons, squirrels, and a great variety of birds. Oh, yes, and horses. Two of them.

The barn was designed to have twelve box stalls, a feed room for grain, and enough room in the hay loft above the stalls to hold enough bales for the entire winter.

There was an eighteen-foot-wide hallway the length of the barn, with two sliding doors at each end. I thought that was a good design, and it proved to be for our purpose.

We needed another horse. Joy liked to ride as much as I did. She liked Candy, the black one, and Silky was Ken and Judy's. So, we went horse-hunting. A few were advertised, so we started with them. None of them were satisfactory. We spent all morning, with no luck. Finally, we found one more to try, and went to the home of a family that were the parents of one of my high-school biology students. They were good people and were glad that we might buy the mare as they wanted a good home for her.

The mare was in a box stall, standing expectantly when we stepped into sight. She was a dark bay, a granddaughter of King, one of the foundation sires of the quarter horse breed. I held out my hand, she nuzzled it, laid her head on my shoulder, and I knew that I was going to buy her. Period. She was priced fairly and we went back to the ranch, got the trailer, and took her home. Her name was King's Trixie, and she was a born champ.

It was early afternoon when we got home, too early to do chores, and I just had to try out that mare. I knew that Joy would want a turn, too.

We walked across the arena and down toward the woods, tried her canter and trot, and I was bursting to let her really open up into a full run, but thought better of it. I didn't want to expect too much until she was accustomed to the strange footing, as she had no experience on hills and rough ground.

One thing I did want to try. I expected any horse of mine to stop when I said, "Whoa," and to stand until the rider cued it to move. So, I said, "Whoa," she stopped and stood still, just like she was supposed to.

We had stopped about twenty feet from a wild blackberry patch and suddenly a quail flew up, making the usual noise. Trixie stood rock still, but looked at the bramble patch with her ears pointed forward expectantly. Apparently, she knew there were more birds, and she was right. Suddenly, the air around us was filled with quail, with the usual noise. Trix stood as still as a rock, I gently touched her with my heel (I never used spurs), and we trotted gently back to the barn where Joy had been watching.

No amount of effort would have kept Joy off of that horse, and when she came back to the barn, we agreed that we had a new member of the family. She never failed us or disappointed us. She died of natural causes when she was fifteen.

There was one other gold mine that we discovered that day. Just as we were leaving the Casella home with Trixie, I saw a Border Collie pup watching us. He was a pretty red and white pup of about three months old. He was wanting desperately to go with that horse! I said something about it to Mr. Casella, and he said, "How about taking him along with you?" I didn't know it at the time, but found out later that the family had some problems and were parting with all of their pets.

We took the pup, Joy holding him on her lap all the way home and long enough to show him the new home. His name was Rocky and he seemed perfectly at ease until Joy put him down on the ground. He was frightened, and ran like scared rabbit out the gate and across the field.

There was nothing we could do about it until we had cared for the horse. We knew that he was too young to find his way back again, and probably wouldn't want to, so after Trixie was safe in the barn learning where home was, I went on a search, but there was no use. He could not be found and I was very disappointed at the loss, but planned to look again later. Just before I got to our road, I saw a car coming out of our driveway and turn down the road the opposite way from me. When I drove into our drive, there was Joy, with Rocky in her arms, and he was wagging his tail to beat the band.

In all the fourteen years that we had him, he never voluntarily left our sight. If we had to leave him, he watched patiently for our return, so he could look after us.

When I was putting the metal roof on the barn, I had to lean the twenty-two-foot long sheets against the barn, then climb a ladder to the roof, pull the metal sheet up, and nail it in place, then climb down for another one.

As soon as my feet touched the ladder, Rocky started to cry, and worried until I was back down on the ground. When he saw that I was not going to quit, he went to the house, got Joy and settled down beside her.

At night, he lay on the floor on my side of the bed, and several times during the night, he would get up, make sure that I was all right, then lay down again and go to sleep. Or, so I thought. I found out eventually the he knew about everything that went on, and didn't hesitate to take care of it.

This way of life was as good as any I ever hoped to live, but there were a few drawbacks, the main one being that we were tied down to (what we called) a ranch, and there were times when I had to be gone, sometimes for extended periods.

So, we took care of it. As usual, there is a way if you can recognize it.

To wit: we had an ideal place to raise horses (a good way to go broke), not only for ourselves, but for sale. That sounded good when you talked about it, but I knew myself (Aristotle would have been proud), and I knew that if Trixie had a foal, that I would never part with it. Therefore, our best interest lay in some other direction.

Two or three people asked me if I would consider boarding their horse. I would, and did. I took horses owned by friends or, at least, people that I knew well. Soon, all of my stalls were filled, I had enough hay of my own to feed them, grain was delivered and put in my feed room, a water heater in the stock tank kept the water from freezing in winter, and I got one dollar a day for each horse.

One of the biology students at school wanted a horse, and when I had a place for it, brought it out. His name was Tom Keenan. He and his wife had a nice trailer home, but had to pay rent for a place to park it. After a few weeks of getting to know them, I asked them if they would consider moving their trailer out to our place, rent free, to be there to look after things and do the chores when I had to be, or wanted to be, gone. They thought that was a good idea, and it was.

The only expense that I had was for the installation of a septic system and power line. We got along fine, liked each other, and the association continued until they graduated and went to Colorado to teach.

Ken was about halfway through his studies for a master's degree when he was called up for duty in the armed forces. He had a difficult problem to solve: be drafted into the service, serve his three years, and hopefully return to school, or to apply for officer's candidate school and serve twenty years.

He elected the latter, and was accepted by the Air Force. He was eventually assigned to the missile school and completed most of his twenty years in that division. Of course, the missiles were no longer required, so his last years of duty were spent in other work.

He terminated his service with the rank of Major, and was hired by the Boeing Aircraft Company where he worked for seven years.

He did complete the requirements for a master's degree in business management and is still living in Wichita.

His two daughters have presented me with three great grandchildren, of whom I am very proud.

So proud, in fact, that when Candace Leigh was born, we made four trips to Tucson and shot what seemed like miles of 8 mm. movie film, mostly of the baby, during those four years. Candace had little baby Morgan Ann now. If Joy had her way, I think we would have moved along with Ken and Judy, just to be near Candy and the little baby sister that caught up with us while Ken had a hitch at the base of Grand Forks. This little one, Beth Ann, now has two of her own: Kain (a future great scientist) and Chauncy, who is too young to pick a profession, but is a veteran of knowing how to get what she wants. It seems to run in the family!

Meanwhile, Joy and I had been holding down our teaching jobs. Mine had grown and expanded, having taken on extra activities such as a State Department of Education representative. I visited schools in the central and north central part of the state, gave dozens of workshops for teachers and administrators, speaking at teacher's institutes and commencements.

I probably enjoyed this, but the workload was beginning to tell. I was in my early-to-mid fifties, and thought I was getting old!

Joy had a bout with rheumatoid arthritis and it was difficult for her to keep up with her schedule. We had also added five registered Angus heifers to our menagerie, and they required some attention, but I didn't mind. I just liked cattle and had been long away from them.

We did manage one more fun thing to do each year. We had a reunion of Joy's family and my family out at the ranch.

Some of the older ones slept in the house. Some in the driveway of the barn, some had tents, and I think one or two slept under a tree or in the tack shed.

Supper on Saturday evening was a weiner roast—baked bean-potato salad affair; breakfast was sausage and pancakes cooked over my large griddle with a wood fire. Sunday dinner was a stew that had been cooking for hours in a fifty-gallon rendering kettle.

There was much visiting and story-telling (some of them true), and accompanied by guitar and ukulele mostly played by Lee and Clarice, a singing of the old songs, and in many instances, the old, old songs. There are few things that can bring back memories any better than the old songs.

Joy continued treatment for the arthritis. There seemed to be something more needed, but none of the doctors seemed to have the answer. Or, if they did, they didn't want to commit themselves. It was another three or four years before we realized how serious it was.

One day, I picked up one of the education journals and was skimming it hopefully, but doubting if I would find anything very interesting.

I did. It was an article on the retirement system, and I read it with some enthusiasm, because I could retire, have a fair income, and still not have to work as hard as I had the past years.

Now, that is something to be considered, and Joy and I gave a lot of thought to the advantages vs. the disadvantages of early retirement. Joy was still teaching, but it was more difficult for her, and rather than wear out physically, she decided to retire also.

We didn't make a large profit from our farm projects, but we enjoyed being outdoors with our animals, garden and the people who boarded their horses with us.

We became a part of the "horse people" group and went to shows with some of our horses and watched them win ribbons and trophies.

Chuck and Yvonne Doman helped with the training and showing and finally, Yvonne, who was an expert horsewoman, bought a young stud from us. He was out of Clabber's Annie, who was a granddaughter of old Clabber, a former world champion quarter horse. She was a great cutting horse, and I have seen her cutting calves out of my herd and bunching them up away from their mothers just for fun. It was also fun for me to look out at the pasture, and see her work. She nearly always won the cutting-class show. Trixie nearly always won the reining class.

The young stallion bought by Yvonne was named Clabber Rebel, and had a very good reputation as a trail class. He won first-place ribbon almost every time he was shown.

Ken and Joy had bought a mare called Holly F. Bars. She was shown in both Western and English shows, and did very well in both. She was the one of the horse population that looked after all of the animals on the farm, even the cats. If there was a cat in her stall, she would not move her feet until the cat was gone.

She was good at opening gates, too; almost as good as Trixie. If a gate was tied shut with a rope, one or the other of them would untie it, let the gate swing open, then watch while the rest of the bunch got out and had to be rounded up and put back in their pasture with a chain to fasten the gate shut.

It makes you think black thoughts, and use words fit only for horses; or sometimes, cows.

Annie was the one who liked to try you out, to see how much she could get away with, especially when you were trimming her hoofs.

When you picked up a front leg and put it in position to trim, she would stand like a doll for about twenty seconds. Then, she would lean gently toward you so that you were supporting part of her weight. Then, you pushed her back, and by the time you had picked up your tools, she was leaning on you again. This would continue until, in desperation, you said, "G— D— you, Annie! Get off of my foot!" Then, she would stand upright, and if you worked fast, you could get the hoof trimmed before she remembered to lean on you again. In rare instances, it took a smack with the hoof trimmer to reinforce what you said.

She was not a real pretty horse, but she was good at any kind of ranch work, had a smooth gait for riding, and I loved her, second only to Trixie.

I had not forgotten about retirement, and by the spring of 1973, I had sorted out the pros and cons and made my decision. I would retire, effective in August immediately after camp.

I would be fifty-seven years old, I had spent thirty-six years in the classroom. I had reached the top of the pay scale for my title, I had given all of my professional life to my students and my school, and last, but not least, I was tired.

I surely had a basketful of memories. My classes had always been filled, I had not had to fail many students, and I had made a lot of friends, both students and faculty.

I don't mean to infer that the decision was easily reached, because it wasn't, but I had to think fore; not back.

I taught my last summer session, went to my last handicapped children's camp, and cleaned out my office, getting ready for my successor. I went out the door, removed my nameplate, stuck it in my pocket, locked the door, turned in my keys, and never went back. Did I ever get over the feeling of loss? No. Writing this brings it back and I doubt if there will ever be a time I when I don't wish I could go back. But, I get over it.

I spent three more years on the ranch (we now called it the Redbud Valley Ranch). They were good years, and we assumed that we would spend the rest of our life there. We certainly had everything that we needed to be happy and content, but that was not to be.

Time for a Move

I had built a nucleus of a little cattle herd with the purchase of five registered Angus heifers and had good luck with them, especially after I discovered that I had to cut back on the feed to my producing heifers and cows. I was having too much trouble with birthing the oversized calves. I had to pen them part of the day to keep them off the rich pasture. Our family veterinary put this way: "Harry, you are killing them with kindness. Keep them looking so thin that you are ashamed for your neighbors to see them. Then, you won't have any trouble." I knew that, but it was always difficult for me to leave them hungry. I got over it, as you always can with problems that have to be solved to keep from getting hurt.

For years after that, I had little trouble with the cows calving. However, there was never a time during the calving season when you can ignore the possibility of a problem. Neglect is one of the two greatest factors in breaking cattlemen. The other is ignorance.

There came a time when I realized that I had too many head of livestock for the number of acres that I had for pasture and hay. One or the other had to give. Get more hay, or cut down on the number of animals. I bought hay, and what was "cut down" was the amount of profit.

I spent some time talking it over with Joy. We decided that we would limit the number of cows rather that horses, but hadn't done anything about it when events took another turn, and eventually, another possibility developed: someone wanted our little farm.

This was a situation that we had not even dreamed about, and my first response was that we were very happy here, and did not want to leave or to go to the work of fixing up another retirement home.

The man said that he would like to make us an offer, then we could have some time to think about it and make a decision.

He made the offer to me, at that time, a staggering amount. When Joy and I were discussing it that night, I remembered saying "We can't afford to live here."

We were given plenty of time to look for another place, but there was none available that we liked, a situation that made our minds start wandering again. The first place that arose in our minds was the Texas Hill Country, a place where I had always wanted to live. We knew Texas pretty well, and I thought that with the sale money, we would replace it with something similar.

We went to the Hill Country, trying to find a realtor or an agriculture advisor. No deal. We finally tried the local newspaper. No ads.

We spent two or three days hunting and the only thing that we found was the Pedernales River and the Lyndon B. Johnson's LBJ Ranch. We decided to see if they were entertaining today, but were astonished to find a guard at the gate who seemed to think that we were as stupid as we could get. Only then did we find out that LBJ had died during the night. The guard said, "Don't you ever listen to the radio?" I said that our pick-up truck didn't have a radio, that I was sorry that we had intruded. We gave up on the Hill Country.

I had said that I was sorry that I had intruded, but really I wasn't. I was sorry that the president had died and I was sorry for his family, but the ranch and surrounding country was beautiful and I was glad to have seen it. I don't blame landowners for wanting to keep their property. Anyone looking for a place to live in the Hill Country had better have either a full pocket or a lot of credit! It would be worth it.

We spent a week looking, but it was no use. We loved the country, but we were too old to take over any of the places that we could afford. There was too much work to be done on them.

After a short say in San Angelo, we headed home.

It was then that Joy finally said something that I finally realized that she had in her head for quite a while: "Let's go back through Southern Illinois!" We did.

We drove around for a day, looking for possibilities, and finally ended up in Vienna. A realtor there showed us two or three possibilities, any one of which could have been a choice, but always something in the back of my mind seemed to say, *Wait*.

We found one place with a small but very nice brick house and a good shed that could be used for a barn, but the owner wanted to sell and give possession right away. We had not closed on the place yet, and didn't have the ready money, as we wanted to pay cash. If we got the money before he had a buyer, we could get it.

In just a day or two, he called us and told us that the place was sold, but that he knew of a place that he thought we would like.

We left the next morning, going back to the place that we had almost got. The man called for an appointment with Bob Harper, told us how to get there, and said, "It is between Vienna and Harper's stockyard."

You can believe we drove slowly, studying each place as we drove along, wondering, *Is that it?* There were several farmsteads along the road, and any one of them looked better to us than anything we had seen before. I can remember passing the house and Joy saying, "It would be nice if it would be that one." We never dreamed that it would be. It was.

We got to the stockyard a little before four P.M. We liked Bob right off, and also his wife, Mary, whom Bob had called to go with us to see the place.

They gave a the grand tour, explained a few things about it, and reluctantly, the lady who was renting the house let us peek inside to see what we were buying. They didn't want to move, and I didn't blame them. When we got back to the stockyard (sale barn), Bob called the owner, arranged for an earnest payment, and I breathed a sigh of relief. By five-thirty, we had bought it. It took a little over an hour and a half to make all of the arrangements. I have never regretted it for a minute, and neither did Joy.

We had to move two hundred and fifty miles south, and I made twenty-two trips with our little Chevy truck and horse trailer. Neighbors from up north trailered the livestock and the man who bought Redbud moved our tractor and other implements. At this "point in time," it looks as if that was my last move. I sincerely hope so.

We had bought the farm on the fourth day of November 1976, and since there is rarely any severe wintery weather in November, I was confident that we could get moved before mid-December. We did well with our preparations and after keeping the road pretty hot between Carlock, in Woodford County, and Vienna and Tunnel Hill in Johnson County, we were ready for the closing and to take up residence at the Tunnel Hill address. We were fully established, except for a few items from one bedroom which I planned to get after Christmas.

One time when I was on a canoe trip, I noticed a board and tar-paper shack that had been built on the bank of the river. There was a sign painted on a board and nailed to a nearby tree, saying DUNMOVIN. I knew how the owner of that shack felt. I hoped that I was "Done Movin," too. I had enough of it.

Ken and his family were spending Christmas with us, and we were all together for our first weekend in the house by Christmas Eve. The temperature was below zero and we had a six-inch-deep white Christmas. On New Year's Day, it was below zero, but Ken and I made our last trip to Carlock to get the last of the furniture. We had the pick-up and horse trailer, with the heater wide open and still cold. We stopped in Effingham for gasoline and coffee and were not surprised when the station attendant said that the low that night was $-24°$. We got back late that night, as we had to break ice for the stock to water at the pasture pond.

Some of our neighbors laughingly accused us of bringing the severe weather with us from the north.

Ken and Judy were pleased with the farm, but I think that Candy and Beth liked the old one better. I think that Joy, too, had trouble leaving the Carlock place. It was so nice and we had worked so hard to develop it.

With the oncoming of spring, there was the usual fence repair and other maintenance jobs on both the farm and the buildings, but I won out on that score! If there was a construction fault, it was not of my doing! I hadn't built it. At Carlock, any construction error was mine, and I had no way to deny it!

I soon had the cattle on pasture. I found that we had plenty of green grass by the first of April, a full month earlier than we had up north. I also had to plan for the winter supply of hay.

I found a man who could cut, rake, and bale the hay, but I had to hire a crew of boys to bring it into the shed and stack it. There was an old building on the place that had once been a fruit packing shed when the farm was in apple and peach trees. The old shed leaked like a sieve, and try as hard as I could, I never could stop all of the leaks. Finally, I just gave up and decided to find someone who had a machine that made the big round bales.

One morning, I was talking to some of the men, and Bob Harper said that he was getting a new bailer that baled the round bales, and that we could stop worrying about it. That was good news for me and for several neighbors as well.

I bought a tractor with a hydraulic lift, and for years, I used my tractor to rake, neighbor and friend Loree Harper ran the bailer, and Daryl Cavitt mowed. Bob, when he could tear himself away from his business, helped, and after the hay was baled, Kelly Harper and I hauled it in to be stacked.

We harvested the hay on our own places and sometimes helped other farmers in the neighborhood. It was pleasant work and we had a good relationship with each other (most of the time). It was usually finished by the fourth of July.

I was building up my herd of Angus cattle and decided that I was not going to produce registered breeding stock as I could not put in the time attending shows and having sales that I would have to do to be successful. Instead, I bred my cows to calve in the spring, let them nurse and eat grass and supplements during the winter and the following spring, then sold them as "long yearlings" the next fall. I kept Angus cows, but tried to use a Hereford bull. The meat packers liked that black whiteface and so did the stock feeders.

I had a nephew (by marriage) that bought my steers one year. The growth rate was so good that he placed an order for all of my steers.

We had a lot of company that first year. All of the family was interested in us, but when they found out what southern Illinois was like, they came down to enjoy it. We had everything here that we had up north, only a little more than twice as much of it. Up north, I had eighty acres, and here I had a little over two hundred, all hills, trees, and grass. I loved it then and still do.

Joy got through the summer of 1997 with only minor problems with the arthritis, but she seemed to be failing through the winter. She never let up trying to do anything that would please or help us, staying with me a lot of the time when I was working outdoors.

Finally, spring came, and by May, things are beginning to be very green, flowers are blooming and farm work was well underway. This year, we did not respond and one morning, Joy turned to me and said, "I am not looking forward to this." I am sure that she knew some things that I did not, but it was apparent that she was very ill.

Our doctor put her in the hospital at Marion, then she was transferred to Carbondale. On the fourth morning when I got to the hospital, I was told that she had been transferred to Barnes Hospital in St. Louis.

I drove as fast as the little truck would go, found her, and as soon as possible, she was put in intensive care. I called Ken and Judy, who caught a plane to St. Louis to be with her.

On the sixth of June, Joy died. She was laid to rest in the cemetery at our little country church in Reynoldsburg.

We had been married for forty years. The future without her did not look bright, but I was so grateful that I still had Kenny and his family, even though they were far away.

Perhaps this next comment is not appropriate for this time and place, but I will include it because I must. After the funeral service, the procession passed our house on the way to Reynoldsburg. I remember thinking, *How can I stand to take her past our home for the last time?*

I do not remember anything at all about the funeral, and the lunch served at our house for those who were far from home. I had completely blacked out.

One thing that I do remember, and always will, is how thoughtful and helpful the neighbors were. There were dishes and dishes of food brought to the house to serve the relatives and friends, offers of lodging, if any was needed, and just all kinds of friendly gestures that helped to pave the way to adjusting to a new kind of life. I learned the value of the "little things," as well as the big. I knew that I was among friends who would get to be like brothers and sisters . . . and they have.

It was easy for me to keep busy. I had four horses plus a pony that was originally bought for Joy's sister's daughter, Elinor Schmidgall, but she had outgrown her and had a real horse.

I seldom rode, only occasionally, to check the cattle. It was so much easier to ride the little I. H. cub tractor and I could haul blocks of salt or other materials on it.

I did, however, have five dogs. Rocky, of course, and a red Australian Shepherd, named Taco. They had provided me with a litter, of which we kept Punto. We had a visit from a traveling salesman one night, resulting in another litter from which we kept Pedro.

The fifth, Kia, was Ken and Judy's Irish Setter that could no longer compete in the shows.

After moving the cattle from one pasture to another, or bringing them up to the corrals, I became aware that I had help. I never worked the cattle without the dogs, and occasionally had told one of them to get "that cow," pointing to the cow in question. I began to pay more attention. In fact, a *lot* more. Those dogs were moving the herd on their own, only needing to be told where they were to go.

Rocky was the "point," leading the herd. Taco and Pedro worked the sides to keep them in line or nipping a heel if one of them didn't move fast enough.

Where was Punto? Punto was scared to death of them big old cows, and took a position some distance away to supervise. I didn't make an issue of it, but, eventually, caught on. Punto would bark if one of the cows tried to leave the herd, and either Pedro or Taco would drive the cow back into the procession. Well, Hooray! But wait! It took me a while to learn that Punto was telling *which* dog to get the cow!

By the end of the summer, I could walk with Rocky or ride the little tractor, and lead that herd wherever I wanted them. No wonder I loved them. I have had other dogs since; strays that someone dropped off here to get rid of them, and all good dogs for pets, but I have never had one that would take the place of those I raised and trained.

My cattle were doing well. I kept all of the heifer calves for breeding stock, not cutting out any of them until I had the thirty-five producing cows that I could keep and produce enough hay to feed. The bulls were a different story. They were sold as feeders, and, of course, were the only income-producing sales. Consequently, there were lean years in my cattle business until I had accumulated the balance in my herd that I had been striving for: thirty-five cows, one or two bulls, enough hay to feed them, and the only expenses were for mineral and protein supplement, and veterinary services.

I enjoyed the cattle, especially going down to the pastures every morning (and sometimes noon and evening) to see how many new calves there were, handle them and let them hear my voice, then on to the next if there were anymore. I discovered what most old-timers have always known, that a newborn calf that is babied a little will be more easily handled when it is grown. I was especially careful to try to have gentle cows and heifers. There are times when they double-cross you and become regular outlaws. Those went to market. I believe that is a genetic anomaly. I have, on occasion, needed to give one of my animals an injection, and have performed that little service in the pasture, not in the corral or head chute.

It was a good thing that I had stock to keep me busy. It was a terribly lonesome "ranch" without Joy and there many times when I fixed a meal and then couldn't eat it. Usually, at those times, I didn't even prepare anything, just ate a candy bar or something left over.

I made a few little trips around the Shawnee Forest and went north to visit with my sister or other relatives, but it was difficult for me to be away from my stock. There was one occasion that I never missed, a yearly reunion with our cousins, the Bueskings and the Reels, from the Strasburg area.

There had been several years when I had not been available when I taught summer sessions, which were immediately followed by Handicapped Children's Camp. Now that I was no longer tied to that schedule, I never missed a reunion, which was usually held at my sister Clarice's house in Clinton. Her husband, J. A. (Rusty) Jones, insisted that it be held there, as he enjoyed it so much.

The families were Martin and Bessie Buesking's and Louis and Clara Reel's. Bessie and Clara were nieces of my mother and were always very dear to Mom and to all of us.

It was at this celebration that I learned that Cousin Bessie's daughter, Dolores', husband had died. I don't understand why I was not notified, but I think that everyone thought someone else had notified me.

Dolores and Clarice had been very close for years, and Dolores had visited at our house several times when she was in her teens. I liked her a lot, but at that time, I just enjoyed having her visit, and let it go at that.

But now, things were different. I felt sorry for her and we visited a little more than we usually did. It was winter before I called and made arrangements to come see her at her home in Mattoon. She had her brother, Harold, and his wife, Helen, over for supper and we had a very enjoyable evening. I stayed all night and came home the next day and resolved to see her more often.

Later in the winter, with the snow a foot deep over the whole country, I was working in the shop one day when something seemed to tell me that I had better send her some roses, which I did—a dozen red ones.

I think we both realized that we needed each other and were good for each other. One thing led to another (dozens of phone calls) and finally those dreadful words, "Will you marry me?" The answer was, "I'll have to think it over." Which she did. She went to Albuquerque to spend Christmas with her son, James Van Scyoc, and his family, and when she came home, we finalized the deal.

I went out to Ken and Judy's and had a wonderful visit to Yosemite. It was one of the places on my list that I doubted that I would ever get to see. I told them that I had been seeing Dolores, but did not say anything about a wedding so soon after Joy's death. I didn't want anything to spoil my trip with them.

Frank and Frances Ausmus, close friends of my family for years, had looked after the farm while I was gone. They were moving to a little house, just four miles from the farm, and we were looking forward to having them so close to us.

When I got home, I sent Dolores a note, giving her directions to her new home-to-be, and on the given day, she found it without a hitch. Frank and Frances were all set to stand up with us, the minister at our church at Reynoldsburg was to perform the ceremony, I had the bride, now what to do? Well it turned out to be the hard part. We got rings all right, but needed a license. Illinois had a waiting period, so we tried Kentucky. For some reason or another, (I forgot what) we couldn't get a license there. We were afraid that we would have to postpone the wedding for the three-day waiting period, when County Judge Williamson walked by and waived the restriction.

We were married that afternoon in front of our living room fireplace, but the preacher had to wait overtime for us to get through the red tape.

As of this writing, that was twenty-three years ago. We love each other and have been happy here on the farm.

We managed to keep busy. The livestock was the top priority, but we had a large garden, a strawberry patch, and had planned to plant several more fruit trees. We had chickens and several hives of bees that I had brought from the Redbud.

I was new at the bee business, but had good results from my established colonies and during the summer, I captured two or three swarms that produced a few frames through the summer and had food to support them through the winter.

The calf crop looked good, all of the stock was healthy, we had all the fruit and vegetables we could eat, but we bought our meat. I never could eat the stock I raised!

Early in the summer, we had a little gathering of the clan. The dominant feature was fishing in the ponds. We were going to try all of them (there are four, but only two were stocked) but we had such phenomenal luck from the little pond near the house that we didn't try the others. We caught enough for one good meal and Dale Broughton cleaned them all. Dale was Doris Della's husband, Lee and Bessie's son-in-law. A mighty good fish cleaner!

I didn't lack for something to keep me busy. Every fence on the place was needing repair when we moved. There is probably three or four miles of fence to keep up just to keep the stock corraled, and nearly that much again to cross-fence separating the various pastures.

Every building on the place needed paint and I soon began to correct that situation. I went from one job to another and back again. Variety is the spice of life, but I got a little tired of so much variety, and decided I didn't need so much spice!

Fortunately, we were in a position that is the dream of nearly every person that I have ever known. We can do what we want to do, in the way we want to do it, and are not responsible to anyone but ourselves. I must admit, however, that I am usually conscious of the effect it will have on my neighbors and the ultimate impression that society gets from any association with our part of the world. "Beautiful Southern Illinois" was not whittled out of the rough by people that didn't care, but by people who wanted to preserve its natural beauty and charm. They have done very well, and we don't need any "rotten apples" to spoil the barrel.

In spite of the hard work, Dolores and I had our share of very pleasant experiences, leading to a host of memories. Dolores has kept a diary since shortly after we were married, and in reading over it, day by day and year by year, I was amazed at the number of weekends that we had company. I know that our neighbors had commented about how often we had visitors, but I didn't realize how often it really was, and how wonderful it was to have people want to share our life.

They included friends like Chuck and Pat Doman and their children, who were "horse people," former students who meant so much to me, and brothers and sisters, nephews and nieces and cousins. Of course, most wonderful of all were the times that our children could come to bring our grandchildren (we had two sets, Dolores' and mine), but in our hearts, they were "ours." You may be assured that the deceased grandparents were never forgotten.

There were many other highlights to our life, and we were fortunate enough to have someone who could look after the home and animals while we were gone. One time, my sister Clarice and her son, Norman Earl, came to look after the pets while we were gone. Bill Weinstein, a neighbor, looked in almost every morning to make sure they were all right.

In the years to come, we visited and thoroughly enjoyed, the "Corn Palace" at Mitchell, South Dakota, before going west to Badlands National Monument, (do you remember the famous Wall Drugs signs along the road for miles and miles before you get to Wall?). I wonder if they are still there, and, of course, the fabled Lead and Deadwood, and shades of Wild Bill Hickock and Calamity Jane. Those were the days! I think I'm glad I missed them. I am sure that I enjoy them vicariously more than I would have by being a participant. I don't think I would have lived long. My "draw" is too slow.

In Wyoming, there is the biggest rock pile that I've ever seen. Of course, I am kidding, because the Devil's Tower is much more than just a pile of rocks. It is one of the world's great lessons in geology; briefly, a volcano in which the molten lava cooled and solidified. Over millions of years, the softer mantle surrounding the core eroded leaving the harder "neck" for us to see and climb. Go ahead, don't wait for me, please.

From the Tower, it is a long day's drive to the Tetons and Yellowstone National Parks.

The Ranger Chorus sings: "Yellowstone . . . it's almost like going back home . . . " Indeed, it is. I have seen it often, with Joy and

Kenny and with Dolores, I have been greatly moved by just standing and "soaking it up."

The Grand Tetons, Big Bend in Texas, Denali, and the dozens of others north, south, east and west. The National Parks system was one of the greatest blessings that our country could have bestowed on its citizens. How the angels must have smiled! I feel so sorry for the people who have never made the effort to see, hear, or feel them.

There comes a day when lifestyles must change, and one day, I was made aware of it: it was a cold, raw November evening; a light snow was falling on an already muddy ground, a stiff breeze was building out of the northwest, and a good heifer showing the world and me that she was going to present the world with a new white-faced black calf. *All right,* I thought, *that is what I've got you for, but please get the job done!* But I soon saw that her little world was not all right. She was going to have a problem. In fact, she already had one. I haltered her and tied her to a rubbing post in the corral, gathered up a few supplies: a pail of warm water, disinfectant, and lubricant soft calf rope.

I made her lie down (threw her sounds too unprofessional) stripped to the waist, and went inside up to my elbow. The darned little brat had one foreleg doubled back instead of being under its chin like it was supposed to be. The cow had been in labor too long and her muscles had contracted until they were too tight. I had waited too long. I lost the calf, but the heifer lived. She was a fine animal, but I couldn't guarantee that she would breed successfully in the future. She got up on her feet before I got rinsed off, and went to a hay bale to eat as if nothing had happened.

I went to the house, told Dolores that I had had enough, and that I was going out of the cattle business. Prices were good, up to eighty-five dollars that day.

The next morning, I calculated the value of my herd, sold it, and learned to live on a teacher's pension. None of the preceding was easy.

I was seventy-three years old when I retired from ranching.

I decided to keep the land and home, renting the pastures and hay fields so that they could be made to produce something of value.

Of course, that makes it available to me to wander over and enjoy, and to fish for bass and bluegills when I want to.

The ensuing years have provided opportunities for travel and recreation, to visit with our children and their young ones, to read and watch television, and to try to keep up with the hundred-and-one jobs that are waiting for us when we have the time.

Our children all live far enough away that visits home are limited to one or two each year, but, of course, there are the telephones and the email or fax. Those that are the nearest come more frequently and are a big help to us.

Much of the maintenance work is done by local young people, who help us and seem almost like members of the family. Some of them have gone on to college or regular employment, but have been replaced by younger siblings or friends.

What of the future? No one knows, except that certain events are inevitable. Dolores and I are grateful for the years that we have had together and for the comforts and devotion that we have given each other.

We will ride out the rest of the trip until one or the other, or both, gets bucked off! The plans and dreams in the time we have left will be nourished and evaluated by the memories of what used to be. I do not wish for it to be any other way.